Bilingual WORDS
NATURE • ENGLISH – SPANISH
1000
Jules Pottle
NATURALEZA • INGLÉS – ESPAÑOL
PALABRAS bilingües

DK

Written by Jules Pottle
Senior Editor Dawn Sirett
Designed by Rachael Hare, Karen Hood,
Samantha Richiardi, Sadie Thomas
US Editor Jane Perlmutter
US Senior Editor Shannon Beatty
DTP Designer Vijay Kandwal
Additional Editing Robin Moul
Design Assistance Sif Nørskov
Picture Researcher Sumita Khatwani
Jacket Designed by Rashika Kachroo, Rachael Hare
Jacket Coordinator Issy Walsh
Production Editor Abi Maxwell
Pre-production Manager Pankaj Sharma
Production Controller Isabell Schart
Managing Editor Penny Smith
Deputy Art Director Mabel Chan
Publishing Director Sarah Larter

Spanish edition
Editorial Coordination Marina Alcione
Editorial Assistance and Production Malwina Zagawa

Editorial Services Tinta Simpàtica
Translation Anna Nualart

First published in Great Britain in 2022 by
Dorling Kindersley Limited
DK, One Embassy Gardens, 8 Viaduct Gardens,
London, SW11 7BW
A Penguin Random House Company

Original title: *1000 Words Nature*
First bilingual edition: 2022
Copyright © 2022 Dorling Kindersley Limited
© Spanish translation 2022 Dorling Kindersley Limited

ISBN: 978-0-7440-6448-3

Printed and bound in China

Para mentes curiosas

www.dkespañol.com

MIX
Paper | Supporting
responsible forestry
FSC™ C018179

This book was made with Forest
Stewardship Council™ certified paper
– one small step in DK's commitment
to a sustainable future.
For more information go to
www.dk.com/our-green-pledge

Bilingual WORDS
NATURE • ENGLISH – SPANISH
1000
NATURALEZA • INGLÉS – ESPAÑOL
PALABRAS bilingües

A note for parents and caregivers
Nota para padres y cuidadores

The importance of knowing about nature

In this technological age, being aware of the beauty and complexity of nature is an important part of our well-being. If you take the time to look and listen to what is around you, you'll discover all kinds of natural wonders. Even on a city street, the world is teaming with plant and animal life, and in every habitat on Earth, each living organism is important in its own way.

Young children are natural explorers. They like to touch and smell and immerse themselves in their environment. This bilingual book will give them the vocabulary, in both English and Spanish, to talk about what they have experienced, and build their knowledge of topics relating to wildlife, the environment, and our planet. It will prompt children to ask questions and lead them to look further and to learn more.

I grew up with "elephant" and "giraffe" as familiar words in my alphabet books, but my grandchildren may never see those animals in real life. We have reached an important moment in the future of our planet. The choices we make now will affect the lives of our children and our children's children, so it is important that we are all fully informed of our impact on the planet and what we can do to protect it. This book is a great place to start a young child's appreciation for the natural world and to begin to talk about living responsibly on our planet.

Jules Pottle
Primary science consultant, teacher, trainer, and author

La importancia de saber sobre la naturaleza

En esta era tecnológica, ser consciente de la belleza y la complejidad de la naturaleza es una parte importante de nuestro bienestar. Si te tomas el tiempo de mirar y escuchar lo que te rodea, descubrirás en la naturaleza todo tipo de maravillas. Incluso en una calle de la ciudad, el mundo está repleto de vida vegetal y animal, y en cada hábitat de la Tierra cada organismo vivo es importante a su modo.

Los niños son exploradores por naturaleza. Les gusta tocar, oler y sumergirse en su entorno. Este libro bilingüe les proporcionará el vocabulario necesario, tanto en inglés como en español, para hablar de lo que han experimentado y les permitirá ampliar sus conocimientos sobre temas relacionados con la vida salvaje, el medio ambiente y nuestro planeta. Les hará plantearse preguntas y los empujará a mirar más allá y aprender más.

Yo crecí con "elefante" y "jirafa" como palabras familiares en mis libros de abecedario, pero puede que mis nietos nunca vean esos animales en la vida real. Hemos llegado a un momento importante para el futuro de nuestro planeta. Las decisiones que tomemos ahora afectarán a la vida de nuestros hijos y de los hijos de nuestros hijos, por lo que es importante que todos estemos plenamente informados de nuestro impacto en el planeta y de lo que podemos hacer para protegerlo. Este libro es un buen punto de partida para que los niños aprecien el mundo natural y empiecen a hablar de cómo vivir en nuestro planeta de una forma responsable.

Jules Pottle
Consultora de introducción a la ciencia, profesora, formadora y autora

Contents
Contenidos

SAFETY INFORMATION: Outdoor recreational activities are by their nature potentially hazardous. Parents need to assist and supervise their children for many of the nature activities shown in this book. Everyone should assume responsibility for their own actions and prepare for the unexpected for a safer and more enjoyable experience.

INFORMACIÓN DE SEGURIDAD: Las actividades recreativas al aire libre son, por su naturaleza, potencialmente peligrosas. Los padres deben ayudar y supervisar a sus hijos en muchas de las de este libro. Debe asumirse la responsabilidad de las propias acciones y prepararse para lo inesperado a fin de tener una experiencia más segura y agradable.

Our planet
Nuestro planeta

Earth orbits the sun in space. Inside Earth there is a hot core of liquid rock and around it there are gases, called Earth's atmosphere. Earth formed a very long time ago. Its landscape and wildlife have changed over time.

La Tierra orbita alrededor del Sol en el espacio. En su interior hay un núcleo caliente de roca líquida y a su alrededor hay gases: la atmósfera terrestre. La Tierra se formó hace mucho. Su paisaje y su fauna han cambiado a lo largo del tiempo.

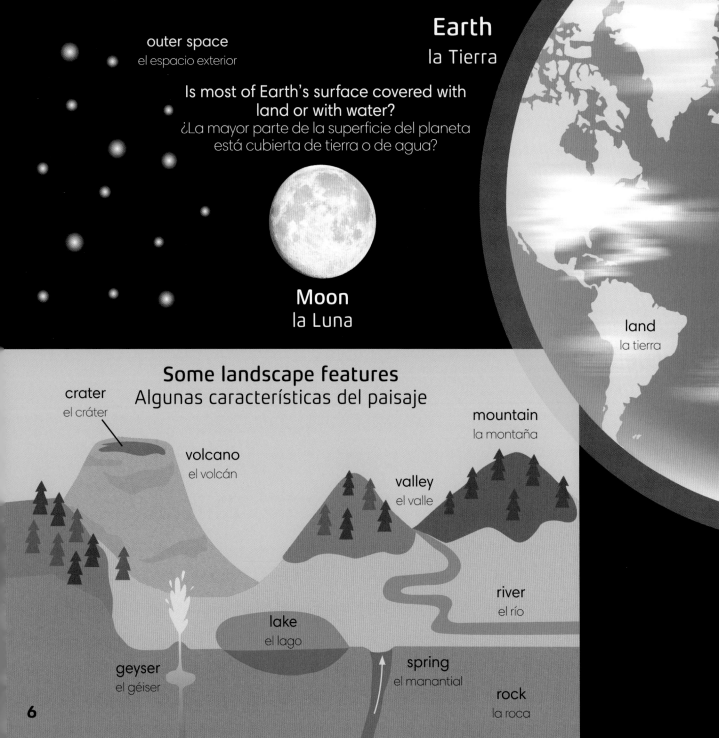

Earth
la Tierra

outer space
el espacio exterior

Is most of Earth's surface covered with land or with water?
¿La mayor parte de la superficie del planeta está cubierta de tierra o de agua?

Moon
la Luna

land
la tierra

Some landscape features
Algunas características del paisaje

crater
el cráter

volcano
el volcán

mountain
la montaña

valley
el valle

river
el río

lake
el lago

spring
el manantial

geyser
el géiser

rock
la roca

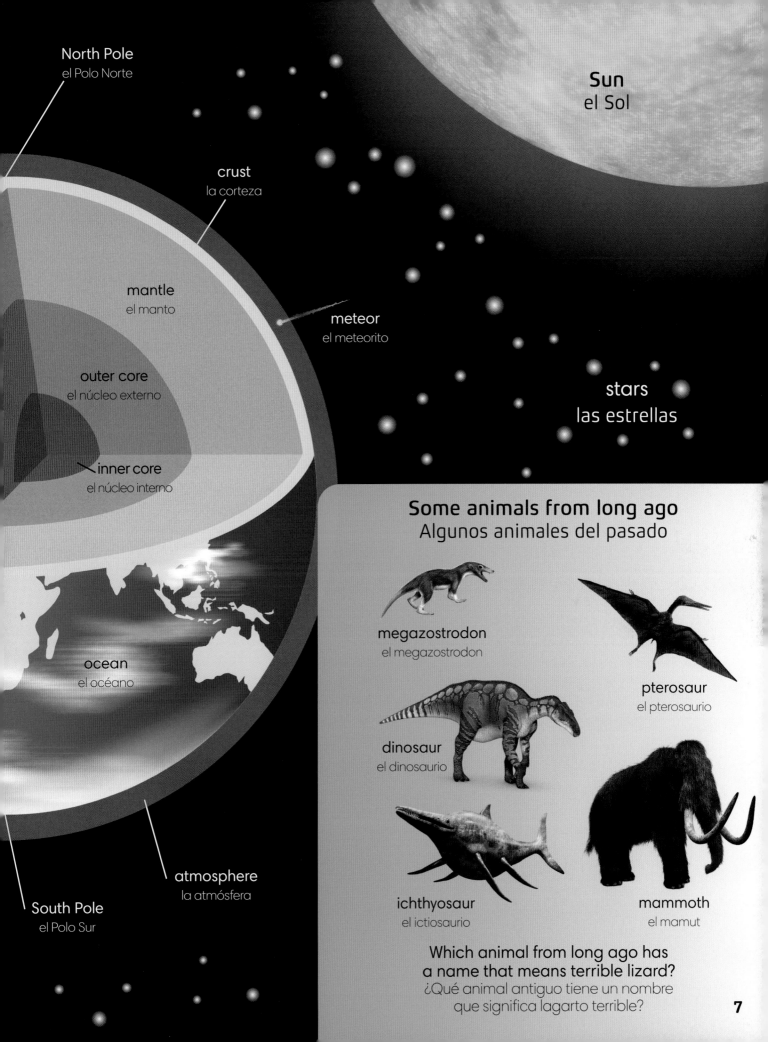

North Pole
el Polo Norte

crust
la corteza

mantle
el manto

meteor
el meteorito

outer core
el núcleo externo

inner core
el núcleo interno

ocean
el océano

atmosphere
la atmósfera

South Pole
el Polo Sur

Sun
el Sol

stars
las estrellas

Some animals from long ago
Algunos animales del pasado

megazostrodon
el megazostrodon

pterosaur
el pterosaurio

dinosaur
el dinosaurio

ichthyosaur
el ictiosaurio

mammoth
el mamut

**Which animal from long ago has
a name that means terrible lizard?**
¿Qué animal antiguo tiene un nombre
que significa lagarto terrible?

7

Our world's resources
Los recursos de nuestro mundo

Our world is filled with useful materials. We must try not to waste them. We also need to reduce the pollution that some materials cause.

Nuestro mundo está lleno de materiales útiles. Debemos intentar no desperdiciarlos. También debemos reducir la contaminación que provocan algunos materiales.

Nonrenewable resources
Los recursos no renovables

fossil fuels
los combustibles fósiles

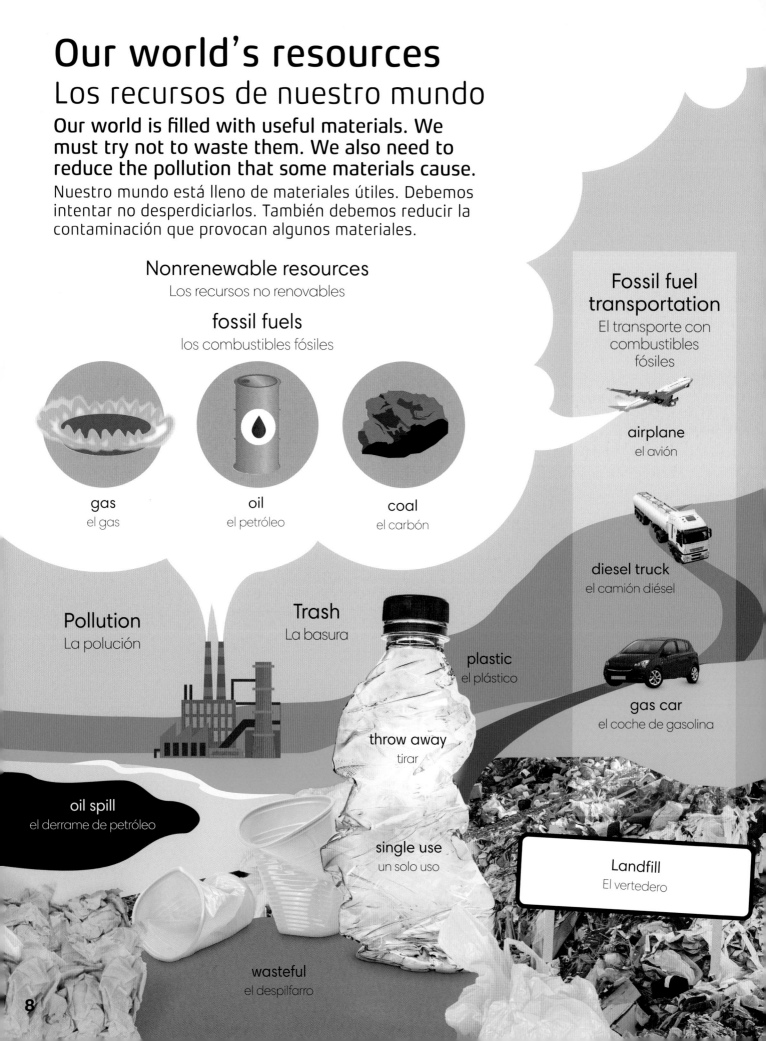

gas
el gas

oil
el petróleo

coal
el carbón

Fossil fuel transportation
El transporte con combustibles fósiles

airplane
el avión

diesel truck
el camión diésel

gas car
el coche de gasolina

Pollution
La polución

Trash
La basura

plastic
el plástico

throw away
tirar

oil spill
el derrame de petróleo

single use
un solo uso

Landfill
El vertedero

wasteful
el despilfarro

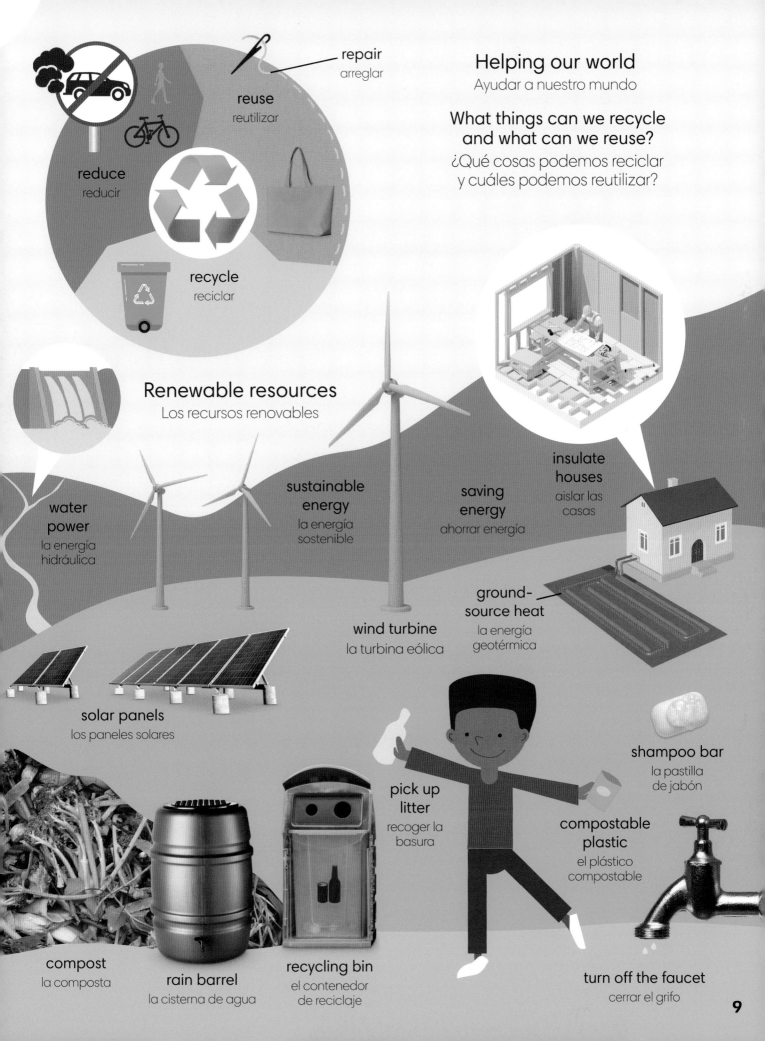

repair
arreglar

reuse
reutilizar

reduce
reducir

recycle
reciclar

Helping our world
Ayudar a nuestro mundo

What things can we recycle and what can we reuse?
¿Qué cosas podemos reciclar y cuáles podemos reutilizar?

Renewable resources
Los recursos renovables

water power
la energía hidráulica

sustainable energy
la energía sostenible

saving energy
ahorrar energía

insulate houses
aislar las casas

ground-source heat
la energía geotérmica

wind turbine
la turbina eólica

solar panels
los paneles solares

shampoo bar
la pastilla de jabón

pick up litter
recoger la basura

compostable plastic
el plástico compostable

compost
la composta

rain barrel
la cisterna de agua

recycling bin
el contenedor de reciclaje

turn off the faucet
cerrar el grifo

9

Humans and nature
Los humanos y la naturaleza

For thousands of years, we humans have made nature work for us. We should do this respectfully, taking care of our planet and the things that live on it.

Durante miles de años, los humanos hemos hecho que la naturaleza trabaje para nosotros. Debemos hacerlo con respeto, cuidando de nuestro planeta y todo lo que vive en él.

On the farm
En la granja

fruit trees
los árboles frutales

wheat crop
la cosecha de trigo

fields
los campos

tractor
el tractor

milking parlor
la nave de ordeñado

cow
la vaca

geese
los gansos

goats
las cabras

grain
el grano

fruit
la fruta

chickens
las gallinas

sheep
las ovejas

vegetables
las verduras

pigs
los cerdos

Have you ever taken care of a pet? What do pets need?
¿Has cuidado alguna vez de una mascota? ¿Qué necesitan las mascotas?

Pets
Las mascotas

kitten
el gatito

rabbit
el conejo

dog
el perro

hamster
el hámster

goldfish
el pez dorado

fish farm
la piscifactoría

beekeeping
la apicultura

bees
las abejas

honey
la miel

beehives
los panales

Unusual farm animals
Animales de granja insólitos

ostriches
los avestruces

crocodiles
los cocodrilos

snails
los caracoles

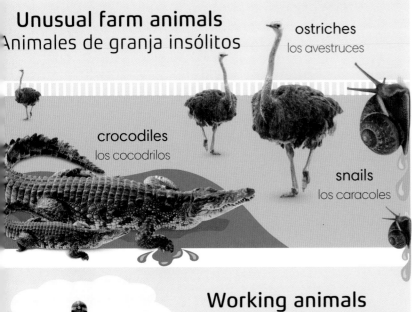

Working animals
Los animales de trabajo

sheepdog
el perro pastor

police horse
el caballo de policía

guide dog
el perro lazarillo

More types of farming
Más tipos de agricultura

flower farming
el cultivo de flores

rice farming
el cultivo de arroz

vineyard
el viñedo

tea plantation
la plantación de té

Farms around the world grow different crops. Do you know what's grown in a vineyard, and used to make wine?
Las granjas de todo el mundo producen distintos cultivos. ¿Sabes qué se cultiva en un viñedo y se utiliza para hacer vino?

Working with water
Trabajar con el agua

dam
la presa

canal
el canal

Mining
La minería

limestone quarry
la cantera de caliza

coal mine
la mina de carbón

11

Nature activities

Las actividades en la naturaleza

There are so many fun things we can do when we go out and enjoy nature.

Hay muchas cosas divertidas que hacer cuando salimos a disfrutar de la naturaleza.

nature spotting
observar la naturaleza

bark rubbing
frotar la corteza

nature trail
hacer senderismo

binoculars
los prismáticos

building a den
construir una cabaña

tree hugging
abrazar un árbol

splashing in puddles
chapotear en los charcos

pond dipping
explorar en el estanque

net
la red

nature art
el arte natural

collecting
recolectar

fishing
pescar

Forest school
La escuela forestal

reading a map
leer un mapa

We could start a nature collection. What things could we collect?

Podríamos comenzar una colección de cosas de la naturaleza. ¿Qué podríamos coleccionar?

picking up litter
tirar la basura

paddling
remar

flying a kite
volar una cometa

building a
sandcastle
hacer un castillo
de arena

crabbing
buscar cangrejos

sledding
ir en trineo

throwing
snowballs
lanzar bolas
de nieve

making a
snow angel
hacer un ángel
de nieve

snow
person
el muñeco
de nieve

Let's choose some things we'd like to do when we go out.
Elijamos algunas cosas que nos gustaría hacer cuando salgamos.

camping
acampar

storytelling
contar historias

stargazing
observar las
estrellas

night walk
el paseo nocturno

tree house
la casa en
el árbol

birdsong
el canto del pájaro

listening
escuchar

looking
mirar

picking
apples
recoger
manzanas

smelling
flowers
oler las
flores

digging
cavar

bird-
watching
observar los
pájaros

watering
plants
regar las plantas

sweeping leaves
barrer las hojas

planting seeds
plantar semillas

having a picnic
hacer un pícnic

13

Weather
El tiempo

The weather is different in different places. Some countries have four seasons; others have two.

El tiempo es distinto en cada lugar. Hay países que tienen cuatro estaciones; otros, solo dos.

What's the weather like today?
¿Qué tiempo hace hoy?

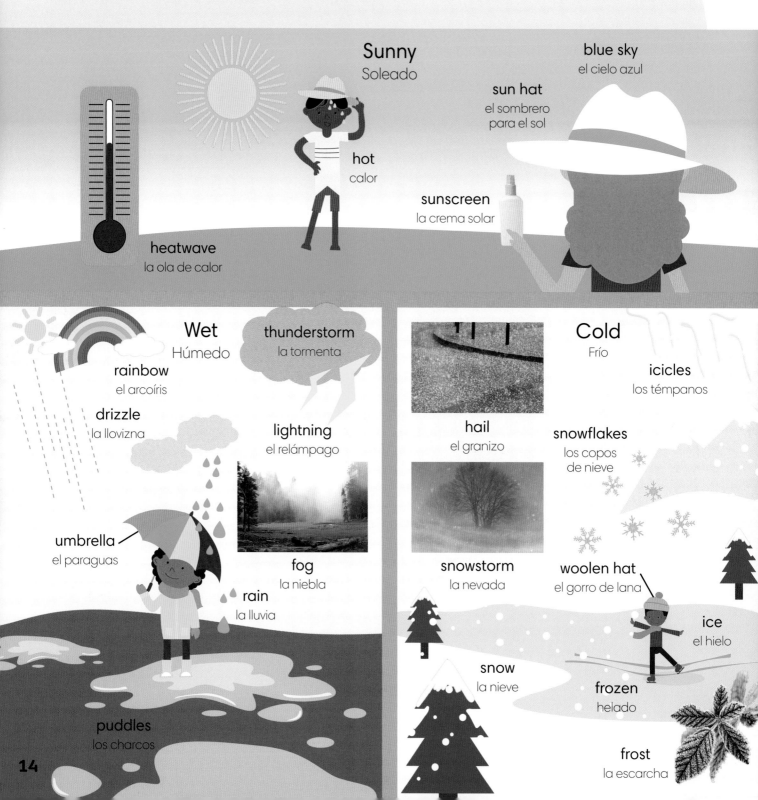

Sunny
Soleado

blue sky
el cielo azul

sun hat
el sombrero para el sol

hot
calor

sunscreen
la crema solar

heatwave
la ola de calor

Wet
Húmedo

rainbow
el arcoíris

drizzle
la llovizna

thunderstorm
la tormenta

lightning
el relámpago

umbrella
el paraguas

fog
la niebla

rain
la lluvia

puddles
los charcos

Cold
Frío

icicles
los témpanos

hail
el granizo

snowflakes
los copos de nieve

snowstorm
la nevada

woolen hat
el gorro de lana

ice
el hielo

snow
la nieve

frozen
helado

frost
la escarcha

14

Cloudy
Nublado

cirrus clouds
los cirros

overcast
cubierto

stratus clouds
los estratos

cumulus clouds
los cúmulos

Windy
Ventoso

The water cycle
El ciclo del agua

Clouds form (made of water drops).
Se forman las nubes (hechas de gotas de agua).

Rain, snow, or hail falls.
Cae la lluvia, la nieve o el granizo.

Water vapor cools.
El vapor de agua se enfría.

Water vapor forms.
Se forma vapor de agua

Water (from rain, snow, or hail) flows into rivers and oceans.
El agua (de lluvia, nieve o granizo) llega a los ríos y mares.

Liquid water changes into gas.
El agua líquida se transforma en gas.

Four seasons
Cuatro estaciones

spring
la primavera

summer
el verano

fall
el otoño

winter
el invierno

Two seasons
Dos estaciones

dry season
la estación seca

wet season
la estación húmeda

What type of weather do you like best?
¿Qué clima te gusta más?

15

Extremes
Los extremos

From hurricanes and floods to dry deserts and frozen lands, our planet has some extreme weather and some incredible locations.

Huracanes e inundaciones, desiertos áridos y tierras heladas: nuestro planeta tiene un clima extremo y algunos lugares increíbles.

Find a type of foggy weather that is caused by air pollution.
Encuentra un tipo de niebla que se debe a la contaminación atmosférica.

Extreme weather
Clima extremo

drought
la sequía

arid
la aridez

flood
la inundación

tsunami
el tsunami

cyclone
el ciclón

hurricane
el huracán

tornado
el tornado

smog
la niebla

sandstorm
la tormenta de arena

extreme heat and wildfires
el calor extremo y los incendios forestales

hailstorm
la tormenta de granizo

blizzard
la ventisca

ice storm
la tormenta helada

freezing
la congelación

Incredible locations
Lugares increíbles

Dead Sea, Asia
Mar Muerto, Asia

lowest land area on Earth
el lugar más bajo de la Tierra

Mount Everest, Asia
Monte Everest, Asia

highest land area on Earth
el lugar más alto de la Tierra

Furnace Creek, North America
Furnace Creek, América del Norte

hottest recorded temperature
la temperatura más alta registrada

Vostok Station, Antarctica
Base Vostok, Antártida

coldest recorded temperature
la temperatura más baja registrada

Atacama Desert, South America
Desierto de Atacama, América del Sur

driest place
el lugar más seco

Mawsynram, Asia
Mawsynram, Asia

highest rainfall
donde llueve más

Angel Falls, South America
Salto Ángel, América del Sur

highest waterfall
la cascada más alta

Grand Canyon, North America
Gran Cañón, América del Norte

longest canyon
el cañón más largo

Kilauea Volcano, Oceania
Volcán Kīlauea, Oceanía

Earth's most active volcano
el volcán más activo

Great Barrier Reef, Pacific Ocean
Gran Barrera de Coral, océano Pacífico

largest coral reef
el mayor arrecife de coral

Mariana Trench, Pacific Ocean
Fosa de las Marianas, océano Pacífico

deep sea
el mar profundo

deepest part of the ocean
la parte más profunda del océano

Which of these amazing places would you like to explore?
¿Cuál de estos increíbles lugares te gustaría explorar?

Kingdoms of living things
Los reinos de los seres vivos

Different features help scientists put all living things into groups. Here are the five major groups, called kingdoms, and some of the smaller groups that are within each kingdom.

Distintas características ayudan a los científicos a clasificar en grupos a todos los seres vivos. Estos son los cinco grupos principales, llamados reinos, y algunos de los grupos más pequeños que hay dentro de cada reino.

Plants
Las plantas

Flowering plants
Las plantas con flores

apple tree
el manzano

rose
la rosa

grass
la hierba

Nonflowering plants
Las plantas sin flores

conifer
la conífera

fern
el helecho

mosses and liverworts
los musgos y las hepáticas

Fungi
Los hongos

mold
el moho

mushrooms
las setas

Protists
Los protistas

red algae
las algas rojas

protozoan
los protozoos

Monera
Monera

bacteria
las bacterias

Mollusks
Los moluscos

snail
el caracol

oysters
las ostras

Crustaceans
Los crustáceos

wood louse
la cochinilla

crab
el cangrejo

Arachnids
Los arácnidos

spider
la araña

tick
la garrapata

Cephalopods
Los cefalópodos

squid
el calamar

octopus
el pulpo

Animals
Los animales

Echinoderms
Los equinodermos

starfish
la estrella de mar

sea urchin
el erizo de mar

Mammals
Los mamíferos

dolphin
el delfín

kangaroo
el canguro

human
el humano

Cnidarians
Los cnidarios

jellyfish
la medusa

coral
el coral

Birds
Las aves

robin
el petirrojo

penguin
el pingüino

Reptiles
Los reptiles

snake
la serpiente

crocodile
el cocodrilo

Amphibians
Los anfibios

newt
el tritón

frog
la rana

Poriferans
Los poríferos

sponge
la esponja

Let's think of some more mammals and some more reptiles.
Pensemos en otros mamíferos y en otros reptiles.

Fish
Los peces

clown fish
el pez payaso

shark
el tiburón

Insects
Los insectos

ant
la hormiga

butterfly
la mariposa

Myriapods
Los miriápodos

millipede
el milpiés

centipede
el ciempiés

Annelids
Los anélidos

leech
la sanguijuela

earthworm
la lombriz de tierra

19

All kinds of plants
Todo tipo de plantas

There are many different plants, but they all do something amazing—they use water, air, and sunlight to make their own food. This process is called photosynthesis.

Hay muchas plantas diferentes, pero todas hacen algo increíble: utilizan el agua, el aire y la luz solar para fabricar su propio alimento. Este proceso se llama fotosíntesis.

Herbs can be used to flavor food. What herbs have you tried?

Las hierbas pueden utilizarse para dar sabor a los alimentos. ¿Qué hierbas has probado?

Shrubs
Los arbustos

hydrangea
la hortensia

boxwood
boj

Herbs
Las hierbas

basil
la albahaca

thyme
el tomillo

Flowers
Las flores

scent
el aroma

hibiscus
el hibisco

petal
el pétalo

bud
el capullo

orchid
la orquídea

leaf
la hoja

stalk
el tallo

thorn
la espina

daffodils
los narcisos

tulips
los tulipanes

rose
la rosa

Guess where baobab trees store water.

Adivina dónde almacenan agua los baobabs.

Weird plants
Las plantas raras

air plant
planta del aire

Venus flytrap
la venus atrapa-moscas

catches flies!
¡caza moscas!

doesn't need soil
no necesita tierra

baobab tree
el baobab

has a wide trunk
tiene el tronco grueso

20

Climbers
Las trepadoras

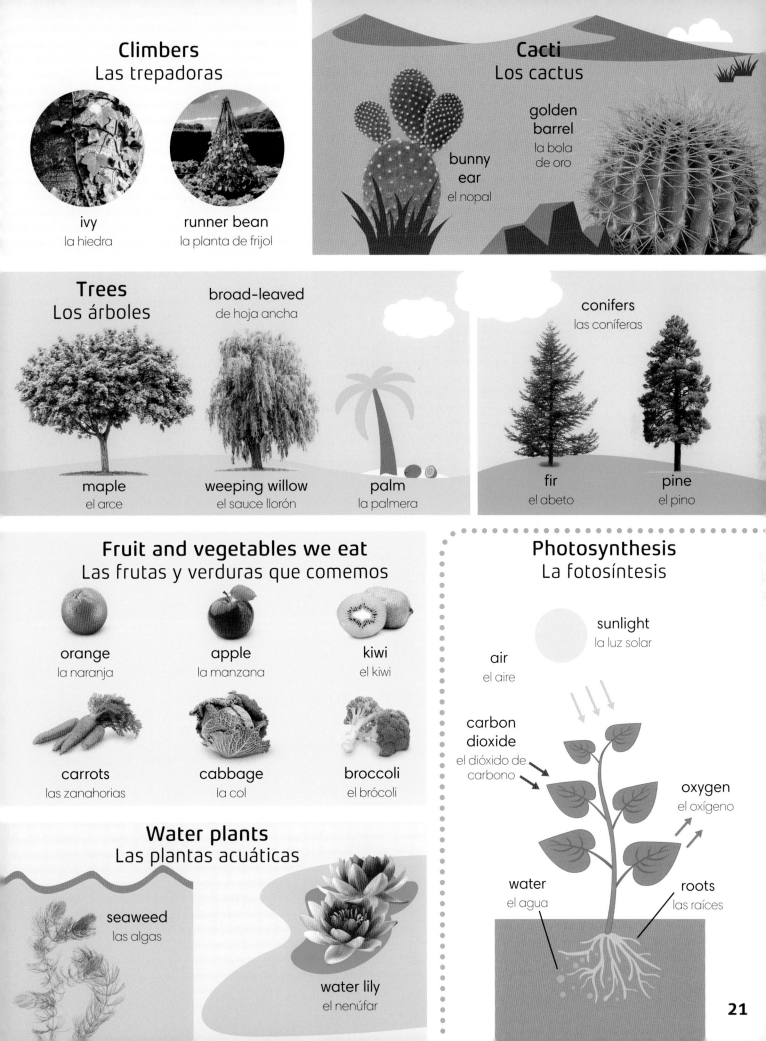

ivy
la hiedra

runner bean
la planta de frijol

Cacti
Los cactus

bunny
ear
el nopal

golden
barrel
la bola
de oro

Trees
Los árboles

broad-leaved
de hoja ancha

conifers
las coníferas

maple
el arce

weeping willow
el sauce llorón

palm
la palmera

fir
el abeto

pine
el pino

Fruit and vegetables we eat
Las frutas y verduras que comemos

orange
la naranja

apple
la manzana

kiwi
el kiwi

carrots
las zanahorias

cabbage
la col

broccoli
el brócoli

Photosynthesis
La fotosíntesis

sunlight
la luz solar

air
el aire

carbon
dioxide
el dióxido de
carbono

oxygen
el oxígeno

water
el agua

roots
las raíces

Water plants
Las plantas acuáticas

seaweed
las algas

water lily
el nenúfar

21

A closer look at trees
Los árboles vistos de cerca

A tree is a tall plant with a thick stem called a trunk. Like all plants, trees improve air quality by absorbing carbon dioxide and emitting oxygen.

Un árbol es una planta alta con un tallo grueso llamado tronco. Como todas las plantas, los árboles mejoran la calidad del aire al absorber dióxido de carbono y liberar oxígeno.

Sun
el Sol

oxygen
el oxígeno

Tree leaves
Las hojas de árbol

lobed
lobulada

prickly
espinosa

pointy
puntiaguda

wavy edges
bordes ondulados

needles
las agujas

Parts of a leaf
Las partes de una hoja

tip
el ápice

midrib
el nervio

vein
la vena

margin (edge)
el borde

stem
el pecíolo

pine needles
las agujas de pino

pine cone
la piña

twigs
las ramitas

The seed of an oak tree is inside an acorn. Where would you find the seeds of a pine tree?
La semilla del roble está dentro de la bellota. ¿Dónde encuentras las semillas del pino?

evergreen
de hoja perenne

keeps its leaves all year
mantienen las hojas todo el año

pine tree
el pino

carbon dioxide
el dióxido de carbono

Tree flowers
Las flores

cherry blossom
la flor de cerezo

hazel catkins
los amentos
de avellano

apricot buds
los brotes
de chabacano

Tree fruits
Las frutas

apples
las manzanas

plums
las ciruelas

lemons
los limones

oak tree
el roble

wood
la madera

tree rings
los anillos de
crecimiento

oak leaf
la hoja de roble

tree knot
el nudo

branch
la rama

bark
la corteza

sticks
las ramas cortadas

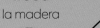

trunk
el tronco

acorns
las bellotas

roots
raíces

deciduous
de hoja caduca
loses leaves in the fall
pierde las hojas en otoño

23

Plant and fungus life cycles
El ciclo de vida de plantas y hongos

Most plants grow from seeds, bulbs, or tubers. Fungi grow from tiny spores.

La mayoría de las plantas crecen a partir de semillas, bulbos o tubérculos. Los hongos crecen a partir de pequeñas esporas.

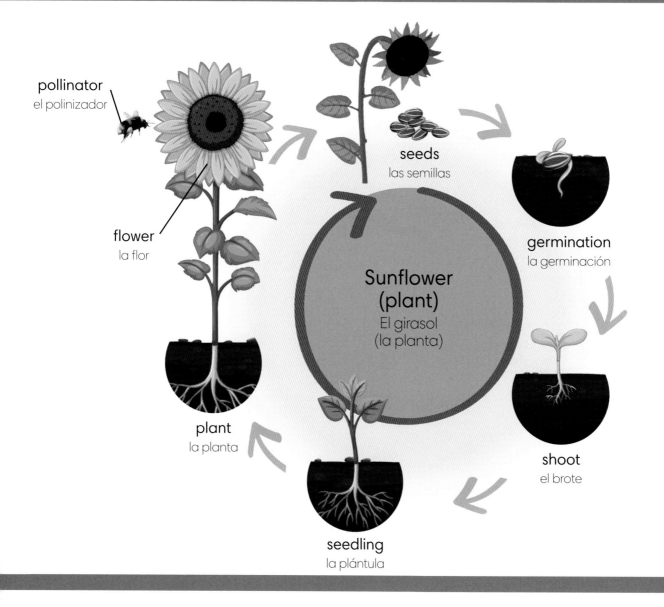

pollinator
el polinizador

flower
la flor

seeds
las semillas

germination
la germinación

Sunflower
(plant)
El girasol
(la planta)

plant
la planta

shoot
el brote

seedling
la plántula

Have you planted any seeds? How did you take care of them?
Think of some things you did to help them grow.
¿Has plantado alguna semilla? ¿Cómo las has cuidado?
Piensa en cosas que hayas hecho para ayudarlas a crecer.

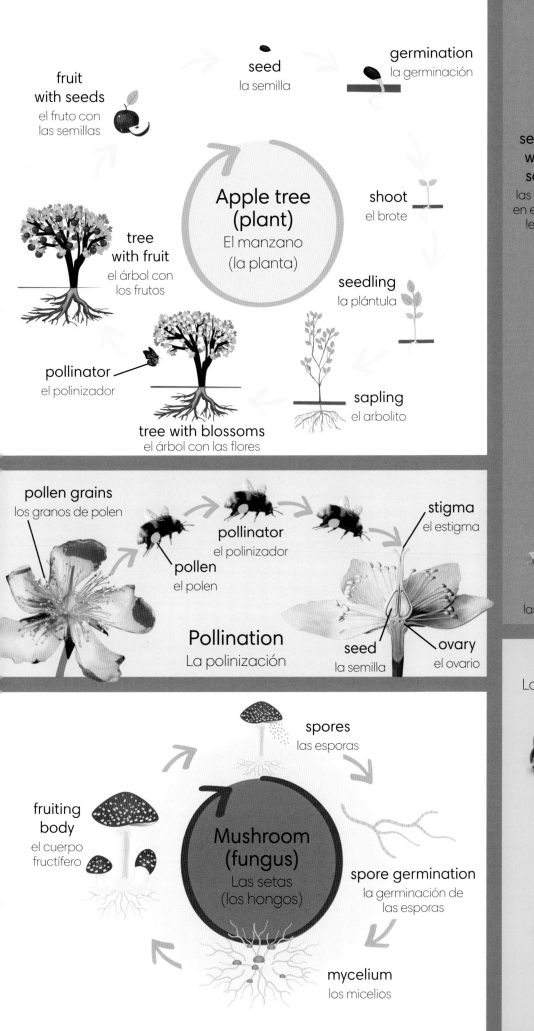

seed
la semilla

germination
la germinación

**fruit
with seeds**
el fruto con
las semillas

**Apple tree
(plant)**
El manzano
(la planta)

shoot
el brote

**tree
with fruit**
el árbol con
los frutos

seedling
la plántula

pollinator
el polinizador

sapling
el arbolito

tree with blossoms
el árbol con las flores

More seeds
Más semillas

**seeds in
woody
scales**
las semillas
en escamas
leñosas

pine cone
la piña

sycamore seeds
las semillas de sicomoro

avocado pit
el hueso del aguacate

**seeds
(peas)**
las semillas
(los chícharos)

pea pods
las vainas del chícharo

pollen grains
los granos de polen

pollinator
el polinizador

pollen
el polen

stigma
el estigma

Pollination
La polinización

seed
la semilla

ovary
el ovario

spores
las esporas

**fruiting
body**
el cuerpo
fructífero

**Mushroom
(fungus)**
Las setas
(los hongos)

spore germination
la germinación de
las esporas

mycelium
los micelios

Bulbs and tubers
Los bulbos y los tubérculos

tulip bulbs
los bulbos del tulipán

potato tuber
el tubérculo de la papa

25

Animal life cycles
El ciclo de vida de los animales

Cats have kittens, and the kittens grow into cats. Then those cats have kittens. Let's learn more about animal life cycles.

Los gatos tienen gatitos que se convertirán en gatos que tendrán gatitos. Aprendamos más sobre el ciclo de vida de los animales.

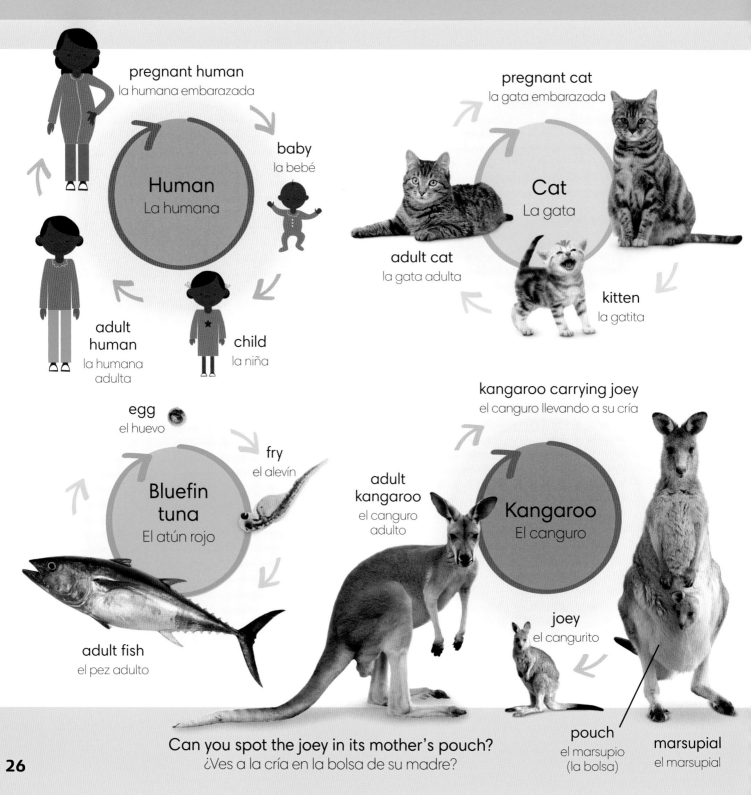

pregnant human
la humana embarazada

baby
la bebé

Human
La humana

adult human
la humana adulta

child
la niña

pregnant cat
la gata embarazada

Cat
La gata

adult cat
la gata adulta

kitten
la gatita

egg
el huevo

fry
el alevín

Bluefin tuna
El atún rojo

adult fish
el pez adulto

kangaroo carrying joey
el canguro llevando a su cría

adult kangaroo
el canguro adulto

Kangaroo
El canguro

joey
el cangurito

pouch
el marsupio (la bolsa)

marsupial
el marsupial

Can you spot the joey in its mother's pouch?
¿Ves a la cría en la bolsa de su madre?

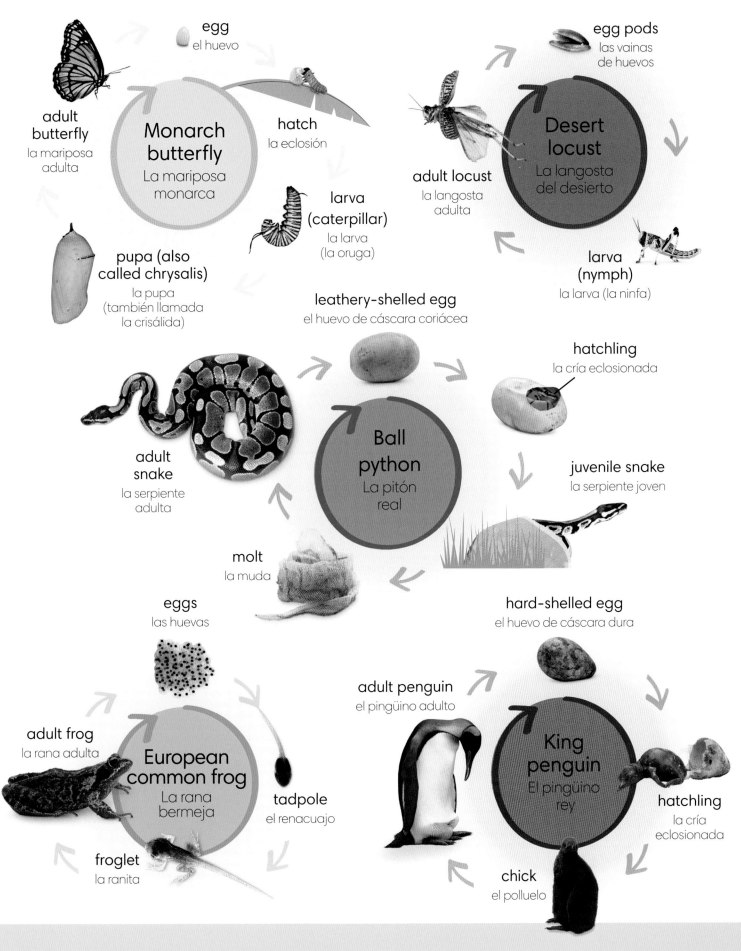

Monarch butterfly
La mariposa monarca

egg
el huevo

hatch
la eclosión

adult butterfly
la mariposa adulta

larva (caterpillar)
la larva (la oruga)

pupa (also called chrysalis)
la pupa (también llamada la crisálida)

Desert locust
La langosta del desierto

egg pods
las vainas de huevos

adult locust
la langosta adulta

larva (nymph)
la larva (la ninfa)

Ball python
La pitón real

leathery-shelled egg
el huevo de cáscara coriácea

hatchling
la cría eclosionada

juvenile snake
la serpiente joven

adult snake
la serpiente adulta

molt
la muda

European common frog
La rana bermeja

eggs
las huevas

adult frog
la rana adulta

tadpole
el renacuajo

froglet
la ranita

King penguin
El pingüino rey

hard-shelled egg
el huevo de cáscara dura

adult penguin
el pingüino adulto

hatchling
la cría eclosionada

chick
el polluelo

Do you know where frogs lay their eggs?
¿Sabes dónde ponen sus huevas las ranas?

Animal families

Las familias de animales

Can you name the female, male, and baby in each of these animal families? Some have special names and others don't.

¿Sabes cómo se llaman la hembra, el macho y la cría de cada una de estas familias de animales? Algunos tienen nombres especiales y otros no.

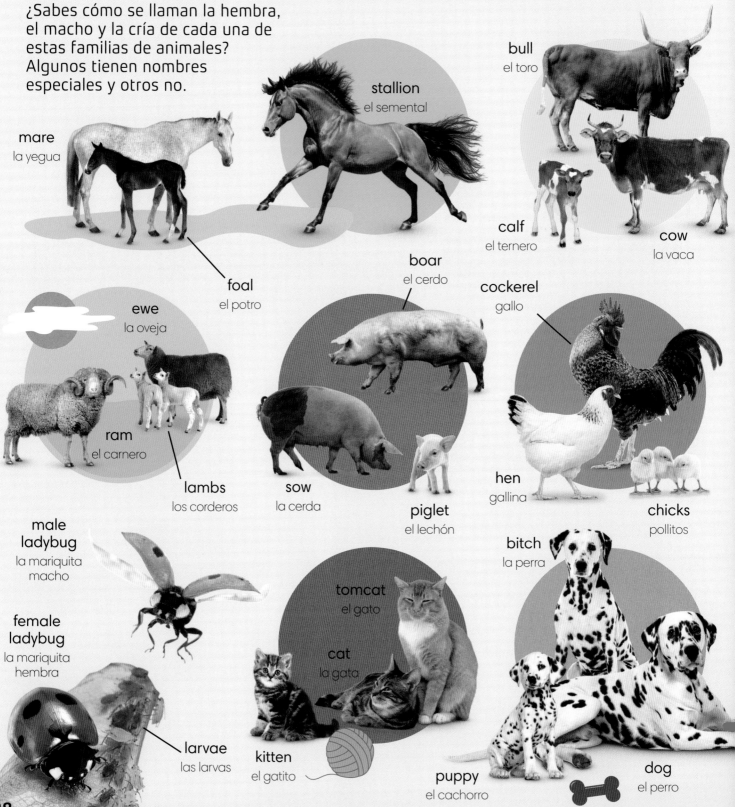

mare
la yegua

stallion
el semental

bull
el toro

calf
el ternero

cow
la vaca

foal
el potro

boar
el cerdo

cockerel
gallo

ewe
la oveja

ram
el carnero

lambs
los corderos

sow
la cerda

piglet
el lechón

hen
gallina

chicks
pollitos

bitch
la perra

male ladybug
la mariquita macho

female ladybug
la mariquita hembra

tomcat
el gato

cat
la gata

larvae
las larvas

kitten
el gatito

puppy
el cachorro

dog
el perro

drake
el pato

duck
la pata

duckling
el patito

male
spider
la araña
macho

female
spider
la araña
hembra

spiderlings
las crías de araña

buck or boomer
el canguro macho

boar
el oso

joey
el cangurito

doe or
flyer
el canguro
hembra

doe
la cierva

stag
el ciervo

fawn
el cervatillo

sow
la osa

cub
el osezno

man
el hombre

woman
la mujer

male turtle
la tortuga macho

female
turtle
la tortuga
hembra

baby
el bebé

hatchling
la tortuguita

Animal groups
Los grupos de animales

What names for groups of animals do you know?
¿Qué nombres de grupos de animales conoces?

pride of lions
la manada de leones

pod of dolphins
el banco de delfines

flock of sheep
el rebaño de ovejas

colony of ants
la colonia de hormigas

Heads, bodies, and feet
Las cabezas, los cuerpos y los pies

Think of an animal. Imagine its head, body, and feet. Are they the same as yours?

Piensa en un animal. Imagina su cabeza, su cuerpo y sus patas. ¿Son como los tuyos?

ear
la oreja

horns
los cuernos

feathered crest
la cresta de plumas

tusk
el colmillo

hair
el pelo

trunk
la trompa

snout
el hocico

eyestalk
el pedúnculo ocular

antlers
la cornamenta

fang
el colmillo

mane
la melena

blowhole
el espiráculo

whiskers
los bigotes

Which animal has the biggest ears?
¿Cuál es el animal de orejas más grandes?

antenna
la antena

wing
el ala

spines
las púas

scales
las escamas

abdomen
el abdomen

Feet (and hands!)
Los pies (¡y las manos!)

tube feet
el pie ambulacral

flipper
la aleta natatoria

paws
las zarpas

talons
los espolones

hooves
las pezuñas

sticky pads
las almohadillas
adhesivas

prolegs
la pseudopata

webbed feet
los pies palmeados

claws
las garras

fin
la aleta

fingers
los dedos de las manos

toes
los dedos de los pies

Why do waterbirds have webbed feet?
¿Por qué las aves acuáticas
tienen pies palmeados?

skin
la piel

Bodies
Los cuerpos

fur
el pelaje

four-legged
el cuadrípedo

shell
el caparazón

tail
la cola

bristles
las cerdas

feathers
las plumas

exoskeleton
(outside skeleton)
el exoesqueleto
(el esqueleto exterior)

endoskeleton
(inside skeleton)
el endoesqueleto
(el esqueleto interior)

Feeding time
La hora de comer

What do animals feed on and how do they eat? Let's take a look.

¿De qué se alimentan los animales y cómo comen? Vamos a verlo.

omnivore
(plant and meat eater)
el omnívoro
(come plantas y carne)

bears
los osos

carnivore
(meat eater)
el carnívoro
(come carne)

herbivore
(plant eater)
el herbívoro (come plantas)

graze
pacer

antelope
el antílope

grass
la hierba

prey
la presa

predator
el predador

cheetah
el guepardo

scavenger
(eater of leftovers)
el carroñero (come sobras)

vulture
el buitre

Food chain
La cadena alimentaria

flow of nutrients
el flujo de los nutrientes

All about eating
Todo sobre comer

mouth
la boca

bite and chew
morder y masticar

Beavers eat leaves, twigs, and bark. They cut wood to make dams.

Los castores se alimentan de hojas, ramitas y corteza. Cortan madera para hacer presas.

gnaw
roer

proboscis
(strawlike mouthpart)
la probóscide
(parte de la boca en forma de paja)

nectar
néctar

suck
sorber

Trap-jaw ants eat other insects.

Las hormigas con mandíbula-trampa comen otros insectos.

mandibles
(mouthparts)
las mandíbulas
(las piezas bucales)

lap
lamer

ready to snap
lista para morder

32

Animals with specialized diets
Los animales con dietas especializadas

dung beetle
el escarabajo pelotero

dung
el estiércol

panda
el panda

bamboo
el bambú

bite
morder

blood
la sangre

vampire bat
el murciélago vampiro

blood
la sangre

mosquito
el mosquito

Can you name another baby animal that drinks on its mother's milk?
¿Conoces otras crías que se alimenten de la leche de sus madres?

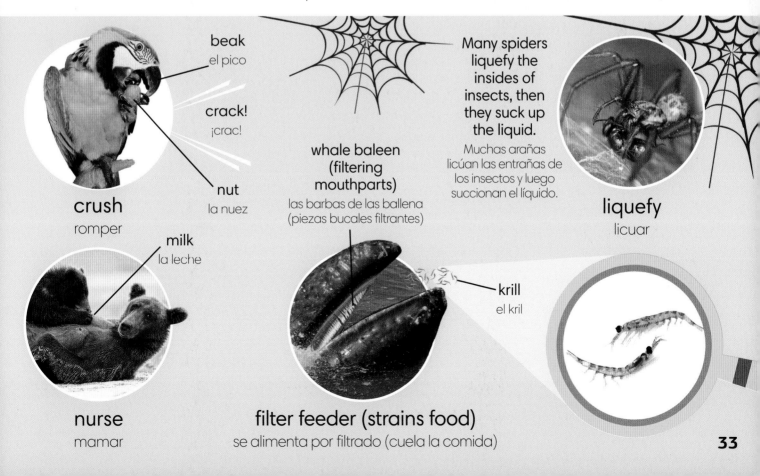

beak
el pico

crack!
¡crac!

nut
la nuez

crush
romper

milk
la leche

nurse
mamar

whale baleen
(filtering
mouthparts)
las barbas de las ballena
(piezas bucales filtrantes)

krill
el kril

filter feeder (strains food)
se alimenta por filtrado (cuela la comida)

Many spiders
liquefy the
insides of
insects, then
they suck up
the liquid.
Muchas arañas
licúan las entrañas de
los insectos y luego
succionan el líquido.

liquefy
licuar

Communicating
Comunicarse

Zoologists can't talk to animals, but they can understand some of their messages. Can you?

Los zoólogos no pueden hablar con los animales, pero sí pueden entender algunos de sus mensajes. ¿Y tú?

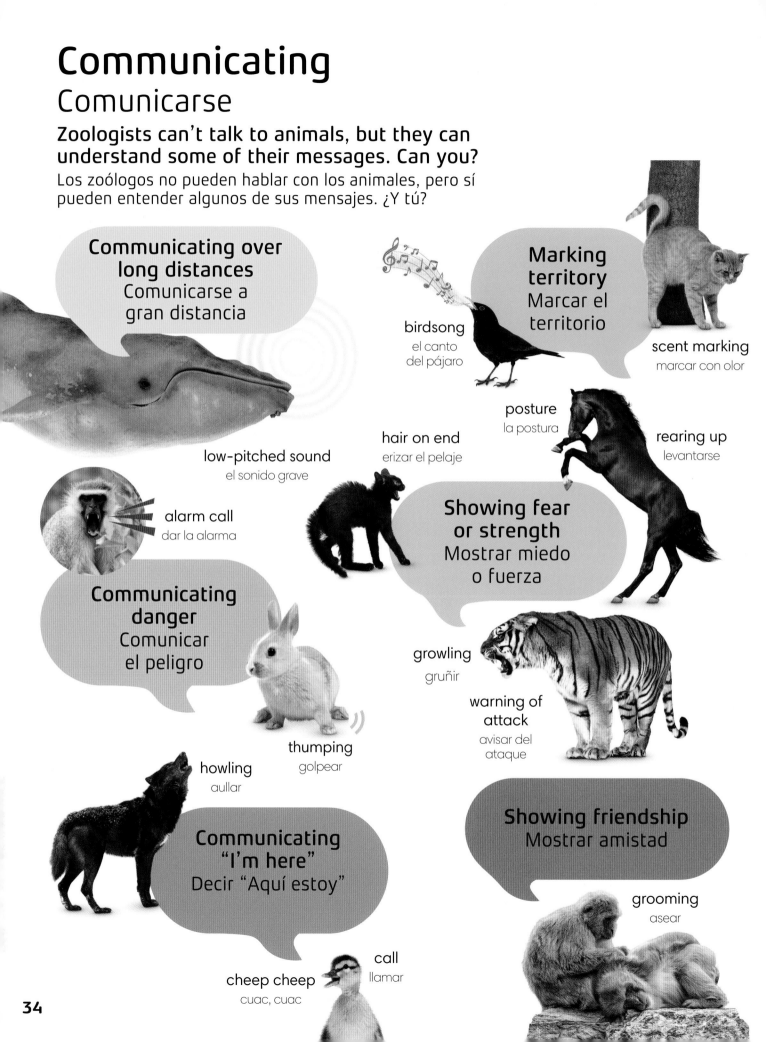

Communicating over long distances
Comunicarse a gran distancia

low-pitched sound
el sonido grave

alarm call
dar la alarma

Communicating danger
Comunicar el peligro

thumping
golpear

howling
aullar

Communicating "I'm here"
Decir "Aquí estoy"

cheep cheep
cuac, cuac

call
llamar

Marking territory
Marcar el territorio

birdsong
el canto del pájaro

scent marking
marcar con olor

posture
la postura

hair on end
erizar el pelaje

rearing up
levantarse

Showing fear or strength
Mostrar miedo o fuerza

growling
gruñir

warning of attack
avisar del ataque

Showing friendship
Mostrar amistad

grooming
asear

Showing where food is
Indicar dónde está la comida

Ants leave a scent trail.
Las hormigas dejan un rastro de olor.

Bees waggle dance (to tell other bees where there are flowers).
Las abejas bailan (para indicar a otras abejas dónde hay flores).

Communicating with humans
Comunicarse con los humanos

Koko the gorilla
el gorila Koko

sign language
el lenguaje de signos

Communicating "let's play!"
Decir "¡Juguemos!"

play bow
la posición de juego

Many male birds sing to impress a mate. Some female birds sing, too.
Muchos machos cantan para impresionar a su pareja. Algunas hembras también cantan.

A male bird of paradise puts on a display.
Un ave del paraíso macho se exhibe.

A male cricket chirps.
Un grillo macho canta.

Attracting a mate
Atraer a una pareja

A male puffer fish creates a nest ready for a female's eggs.
Un pez globo macho prepara un nido para los huevos de la hembra.

Which animal wags its tail to show different emotions?
¿Qué animal mueve la cola para mostrar distintas emociones?

35

wild
salvajes

wolves
los lobos

tame
domésticos

cat
el gato

domesticated
domesticados

sheep
la oveja

Animal comparisons
La comparación entre animales

Big or small, wild or tame, venomous or harmless—just look at all these animal differences!

Grandes o pequeños, salvajes o domesticados, venenosos o inofensivos... Veamos las diferencias entre los animales.

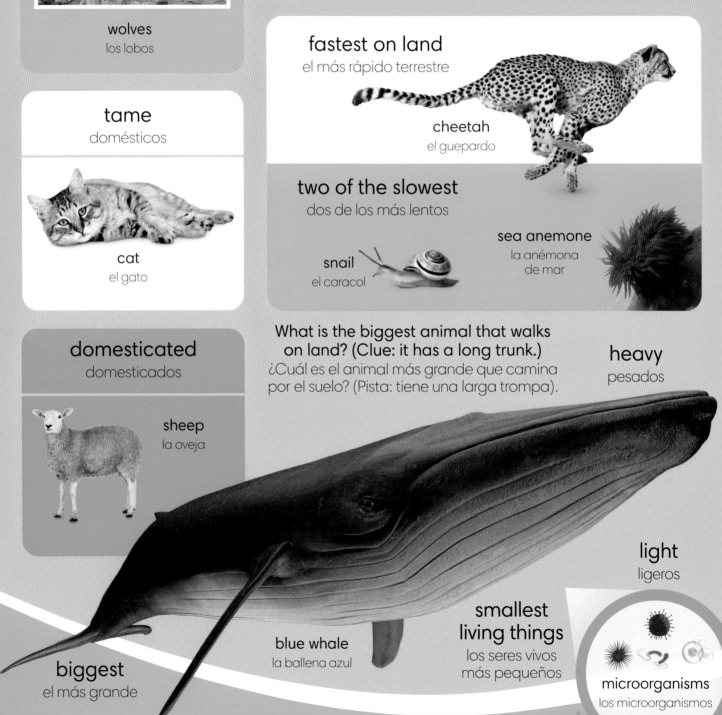

fastest on land
el más rápido terrestre

cheetah
el guepardo

two of the slowest
dos de los más lentos

snail
el caracol

sea anemone
la anémona de mar

What is the biggest animal that walks on land? (Clue: it has a long trunk.)
¿Cuál es el animal más grande que camina por el suelo? (Pista: tiene una larga trompa).

heavy
pesados

light
ligeros

smallest living things
los seres vivos más pequeños

blue whale
la ballena azul

biggest
el más grande

microorganisms
los microorganismos

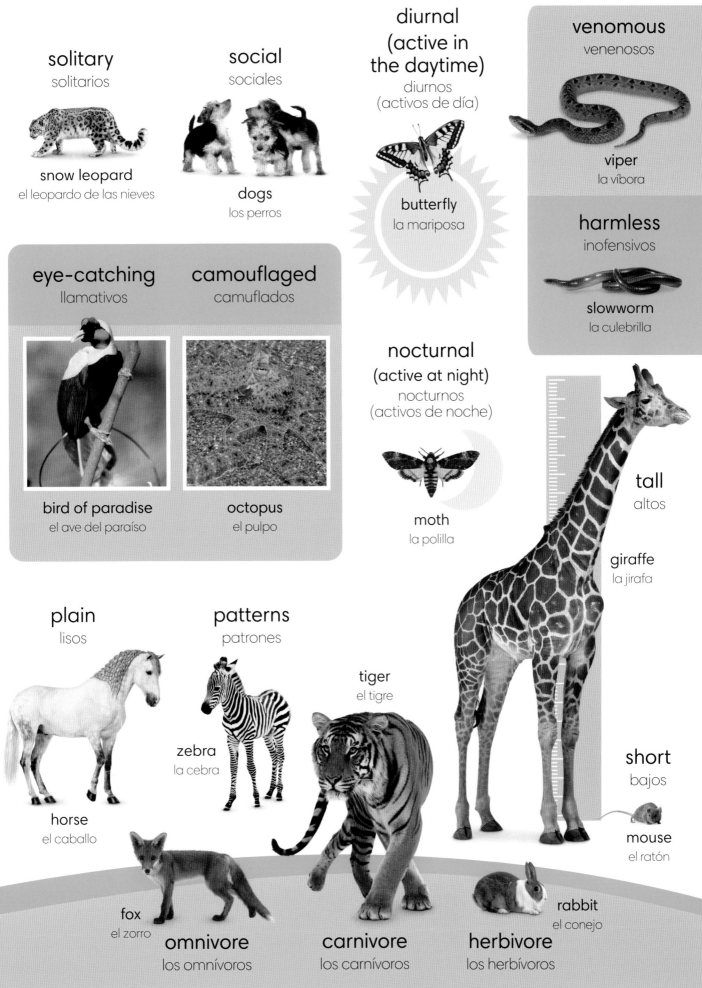

solitary
solitarios

snow leopard
el leopardo de las nieves

social
sociales

dogs
los perros

**diurnal
(active in
the daytime)**
diurnos
(activos de día)

butterfly
la mariposa

venomous
venenosos

viper
la víbora

harmless
inofensivos

slowworm
la culebrilla

eye-catching
llamativos

camouflaged
camuflados

bird of paradise
el ave del paraíso

octopus
el pulpo

**nocturnal
(active at night)**
nocturnos
(activos de noche)

moth
la polilla

tall
altos

giraffe
la jirafa

plain
lisos

patterns
patrones

tiger
el tigre

horse
el caballo

zebra
la cebra

short
bajos

mouse
el ratón

fox
el zorro

omnivore
los omnívoros

carnivore
los carnívoros

rabbit
el conejo

herbivore
los herbívoros

37

Poop
La caca

Poop comes in many shapes and sizes! Which animal has cube-shaped poop?

Las cacas tienen muchas formas y tamaños. ¿Qué animal las hace en forma de cubo?

rabbit droppings
los excrementos del conejo

fox poop
la caca del zorro

bird dropping
los excrementos del ave

lizard poop
la caca del lagarto

wombat poops
las cacas del wómbat

Animal clues
Pistas de animales

Learn to recognize the poop of different animals. Look for rotting plants, too—these are being eaten by animals and microbes. You might also find evidence of things that lived long ago.

Aprende a reconocer las cacas de los distintos animales. Busca además plantas en descomposición, ya que se las comen los animales y los microbios. También puedes encontrar vestigios de cosas que vivieron hace mucho tiempo.

Rotting plants
Plantas podridas

What creatures are eating the log?
¿Qué criaturas se comen el tronco?

microbes
los microbios

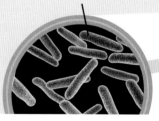

animal tracks
los rastros de los animales

More animal clues
Más pistas de animales

shark teeth
los dientes de tiburón

shells
los caparazones

skeleton
el esqueleto

bones
los huesos

owl pellet
la egagrópila del búho

otter spraint
la caca de la nutria

bat guano
el guano del murciélago

Seeds can be transported in animal poop.
La caca de los animales puede transportar semillas.

worm cast
los excrementos de la lombriz

insect frass
las heces de los insectos

bear scat
la caca del oso

elephant dung
la caca del elefante

natural compost
la composta natural

dead
muerto

carbon dioxide
el dióxido de carbono

new growth
el nuevo crecimiento

log
el tronco

mushrooms
las setas

fungi
los hongos

leaf litter
los restos de hojas

nutrients
los nutrientes

stag beetle larvae
las larvas del escarabajo ciervo

natural recycling
el reciclaje natural

worm
la lombriz

digest
digerir

stag beetle
el escarabajo ciervo

nuts buried by squirrels
los frutos enterrados por las ardillas

Clues from long ago
Pistas de hace mucho

fossil skull
el cráneo fósil

ammonite (fossil mollusk)
la amonita (el molusco fósil)

amber (fossil tree resin)
el ámbar (la resina de árbol fósil)

dinosaur footprint in fossil rock
la huella de dinosaurio en la roca fósil

coprolite (fossil poop)
el coprolito (la caca fósil)

39

Backyards and parks
Los jardines y los parques
There are lots of wonderful things to see and do in a backyard or park.
Se pueden ver y hacer muchas cosas bonitas en un jardín o en un parque.

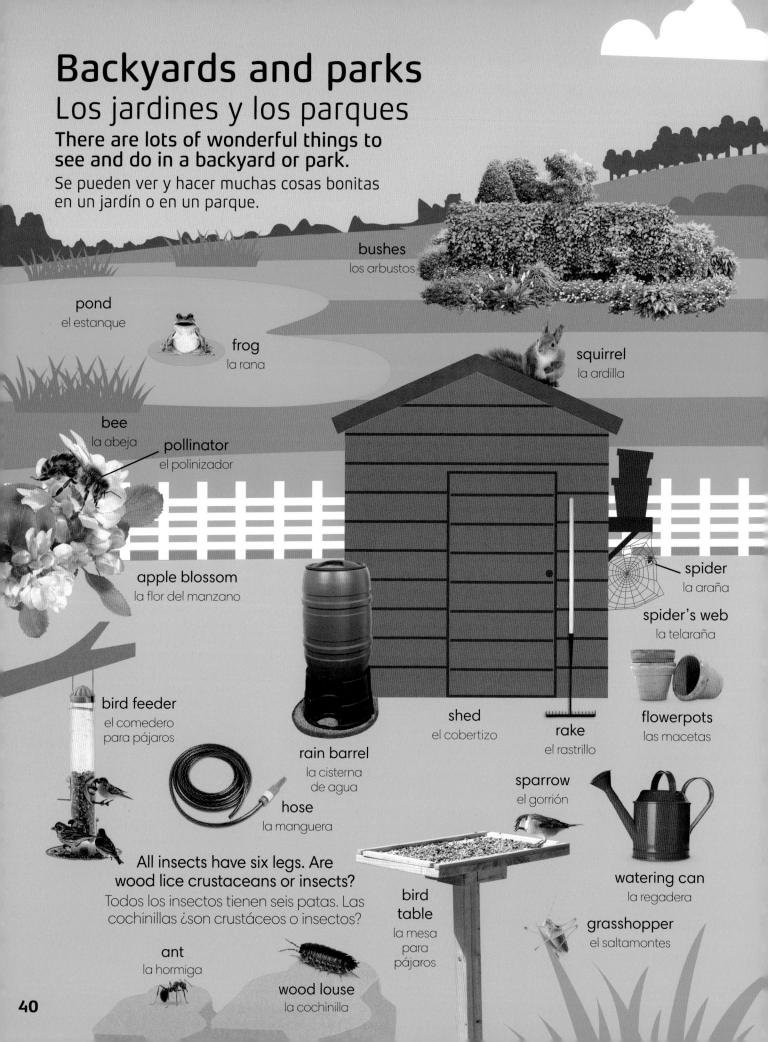

bushes
los arbustos

pond
el estanque

frog
la rana

squirrel
la ardilla

bee
la abeja

pollinator
el polinizador

apple blossom
la flor del manzano

spider
la araña

spider's web
la telaraña

bird feeder
el comedero
para pájaros

rain barrel
la cisterna
de agua

shed
el cobertizo

rake
el rastrillo

flowerpots
las macetas

hose
la manguera

sparrow
el gorrión

watering can
la regadera

All insects have six legs. Are wood lice crustaceans or insects?
Todos los insectos tienen seis patas. Las cochinillas ¿son crustáceos o insectos?

bird
table
la mesa
para
pájaros

grasshopper
el saltamontes

ant
la hormiga

wood louse
la cochinilla

40

Park
El parque

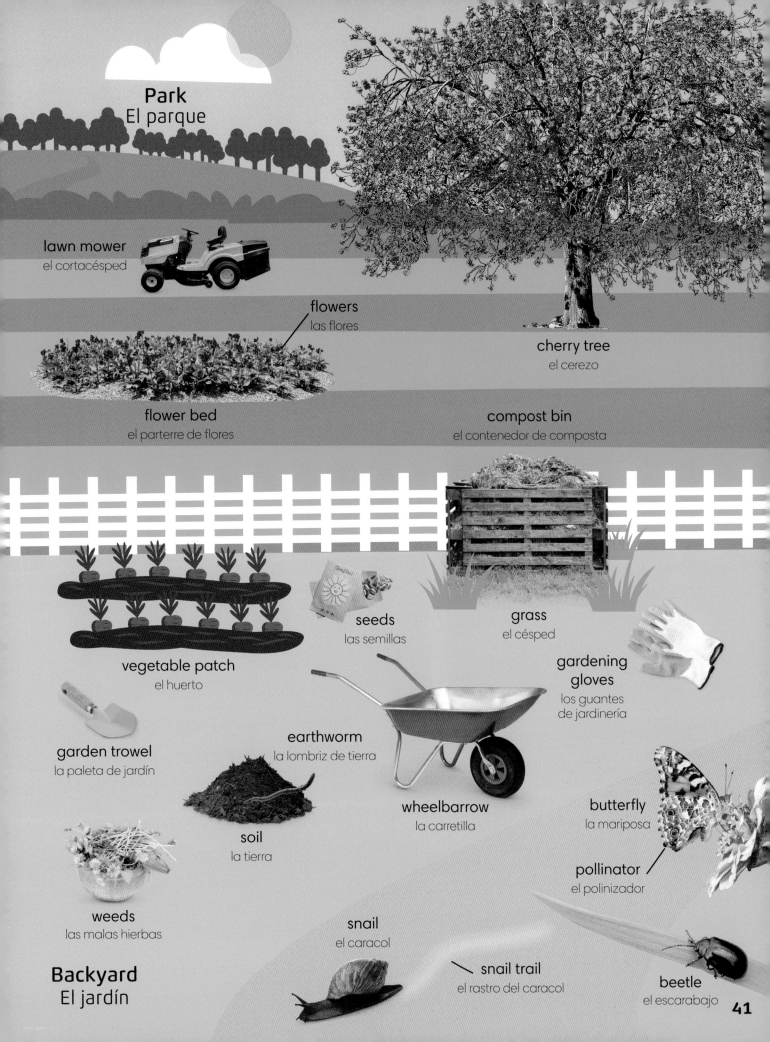

lawn mower
el cortacésped

flowers
las flores

cherry tree
el cerezo

flower bed
el parterre de flores

compost bin
el contenedor de composta

seeds
las semillas

grass
el césped

gardening gloves
los guantes de jardinería

vegetable patch
el huerto

garden trowel
la paleta de jardín

earthworm
la lombriz de tierra

wheelbarrow
la carretilla

butterfly
la mariposa

soil
la tierra

pollinator
el polinizador

weeds
las malas hierbas

snail
el caracol

snail trail
el rastro del caracol

beetle
el escarabajo

Backyard
El jardín

Fields and meadows
Los campos y los prados

Some fields are planted with crops.
Others are full of wildflowers. Grassland can
be green and grassy or dusty and dry.

Algunos campos están plantados con cultivos. Otros
están llenos de flores silvestres. Los terrenos pueden ser
verdes y cubiertos de hierba o secos y polvorientos.

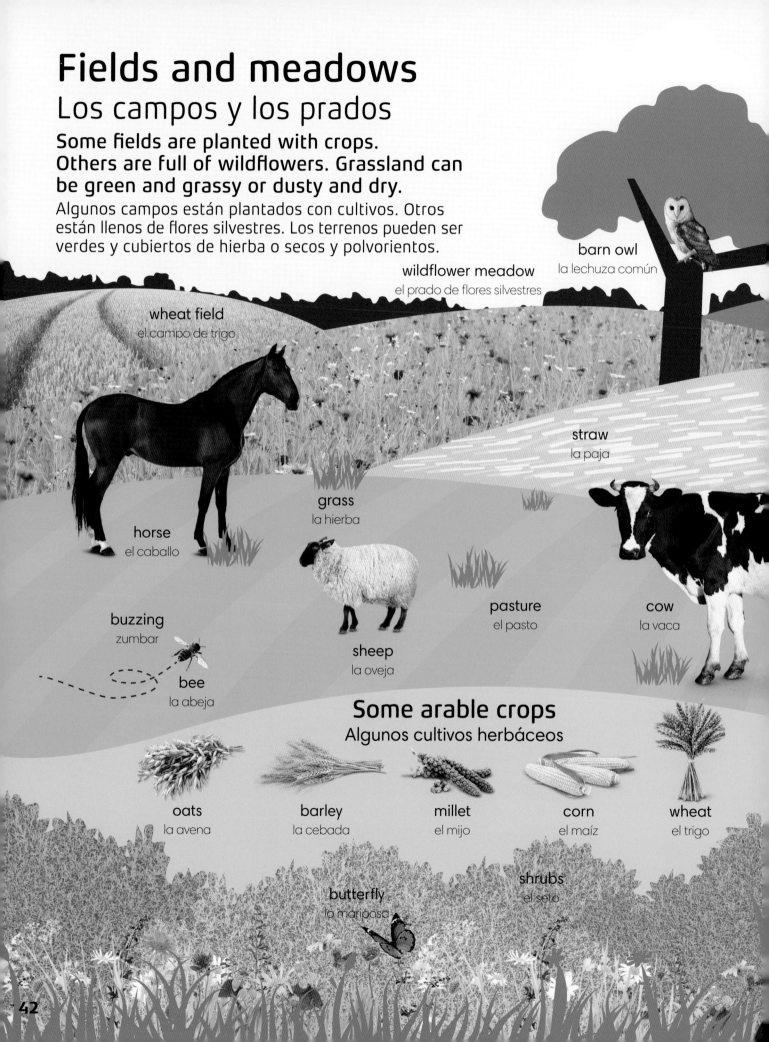

barn owl
la lechuza común

wildflower meadow
el prado de flores silvestres

wheat field
el campo de trigo

straw
la paja

grass
la hierba

horse
el caballo

buzzing
zumbar

pasture
el pasto

cow
la vaca

sheep
la oveja

bee
la abeja

Some arable crops
Algunos cultivos herbáceos

oats
la avena

barley
la cebada

millet
el mijo

corn
el maíz

wheat
el trigo

shrubs
el seto

butterfly
la mariposa

Can you think of a food you like that contains an arable crop?
¿Puedes pensar en un alimento que te guste y que contenga un cultivo herbáceo?

osprey
el águila pescadora

baler
la empacadora

tractor
el tractor

combine harvester
la cosechadora

straw bale
la bala de paja

lizard
el lagarto

plow
el arado

fence
la cerca

gray partridge
la perdiz gris

field mouse
el ratón de campo

grasshopper
el saltamontes

clover
el trébol

mole hole
el agujero del topo

mole
el topo

grass snake
la culebra de collar

mole burrow
la madriguera del topo

rabbit burrow
la madriguera del conejo

wild rabbit
el conejo silvestre

Woodlands
Los bosques

Animals find plenty to eat in woodlands, and protection from the worst of the weather.

Los animales encuentran mucha comida en los bosques, que los protegen de las inclemencias del tiempo.

conker
la castaña

horse-chestnut leaf
la hoja de castaño

conker shell
la cápsula espinosa

chirping
piar

chiffchaff
el mosquitero

red squirrel
la ardilla roja

hooting
ulular

tawny owl
el cárabo

bird's nest
el nido de pájaro

undergrowth
el sotobosque

rustling
susurrar

bluebells
el jacinto silvestre

horse-chestnut tree
el castaño

fawn
el cervatillo

ferns
helechos

dragonfly
la libélula

pond
el estanque

pond snail
el caracol acuático

pond skater
el zapatero

fox den
la guarida del zorro

fox
el zorro

rhinoceros beetle
el escarabajo rinoceronte

European forest
El bosque europeo

Can you spot a baby deer?
¿Puedes ver una cría de ciervo?

44

American redwood forest
El bosque de secuoyas americanas

giant redwood tree
la secuoya gigante

lichen
el liquen

giant redwood cone
piña de secuoya gigante

giant redwood leaves
las hojas de la secuoya gigante

bobcat
el lince rojo

knocking
picar

woodpecker
el pájaro carpintero

black bear
el oso negro

toadstool
la seta

chipmunk
la ardilla

cockatoo
la cacatúa

koalas
los koalas

gum trees
los eucaliptos

tree hole
el agujero en el tronco

common brushtail possum
la zarigüeya australiana

Australian eucalyptus forest
El bosque de eucaliptos australiano

bamboo
el bambú

plum blossom
la flor del ciruelo

panda
el panda

Chinese bamboo forest
El bosque de bambú chino

Rivers
Los ríos

Animals live in rivers, on riverbanks, and on the flat areas next to rivers, called floodplains.

Algunos animales viven en los ríos, en sus márgenes y en las zonas planas próximas, llamadas llanuras aluviales.

weeping willow tree
el sauce llorón

burrow
la madriguera

riverbank
la margen del río

muskrat
la rata almizclera

fishing
pescar

water vole
la rata de agua

Canada goose
el ganso de Canadá

osprey
el águila pescadora

fresh water
el agua dulce

moorhen
la gallineta

salmon
el salmón

carp
la carpa

reeds
los juncos

mayfly
la efímera

pondweed
la espiga de agua

stickleback
el espinoso

crayfish
el cangrejo de río

pike
la agujeta

rapids
los rápidos

current
la corriente

canoe
la canoa

Find the animal in the water
which has an exoskeleton
(a hard outer skeleton).
Localiza la criatura en el agua que tiene
exoesqueleto (esqueleto exterior duro).

open-water swimming
nadar en aguas abiertas

swan
el cisne

duck
el pato

heron
la garza

dragonfly
la libélula

otter
la nutria

beaver
el castor

marsh
la ciénaga

Where does a river
meet the ocean?
¿Dónde se encuentra
un río con el mar?

ocean
el océano

estuary
el estuario

river
el río

dam
la presa

floodplain
la llanura aluvial

waterfall
la cascada

47

Oceans and coasts
Los océanos y las costas

Most of Earth's surface is covered with water.
That is why it looks blue from space.

La mayor parte de la Tierra está cubierta de
agua. Por eso se ve azul desde el espacio.

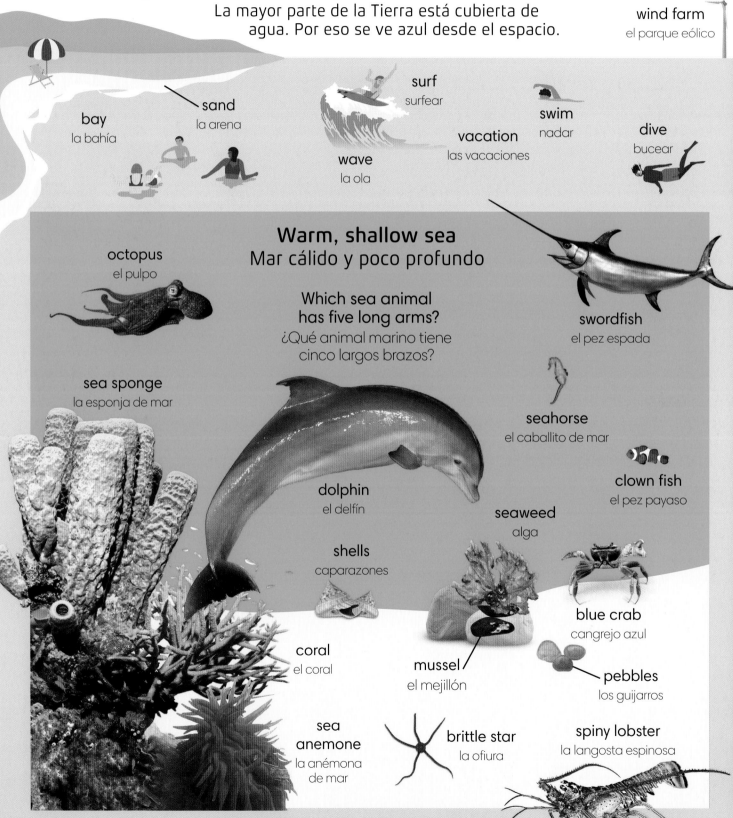

wind farm
el parque eólico

bay
la bahía

sand
la arena

surf
surfear

wave
la ola

vacation
las vacaciones

swim
nadar

dive
bucear

Warm, shallow sea
Mar cálido y poco profundo

octopus
el pulpo

Which sea animal
has five long arms?
¿Qué animal marino tiene
cinco largos brazos?

swordfish
el pez espada

sea sponge
la esponja de mar

seahorse
el caballito de mar

clown fish
el pez payaso

dolphin
el delfín

seaweed
alga

shells
caparazones

blue crab
cangrejo azul

coral
el coral

mussel
el mejillón

pebbles
los guijarros

sea
anemone
la anémona
de mar

brittle star
la ofiura

spiny lobster
la langosta espinosa

48

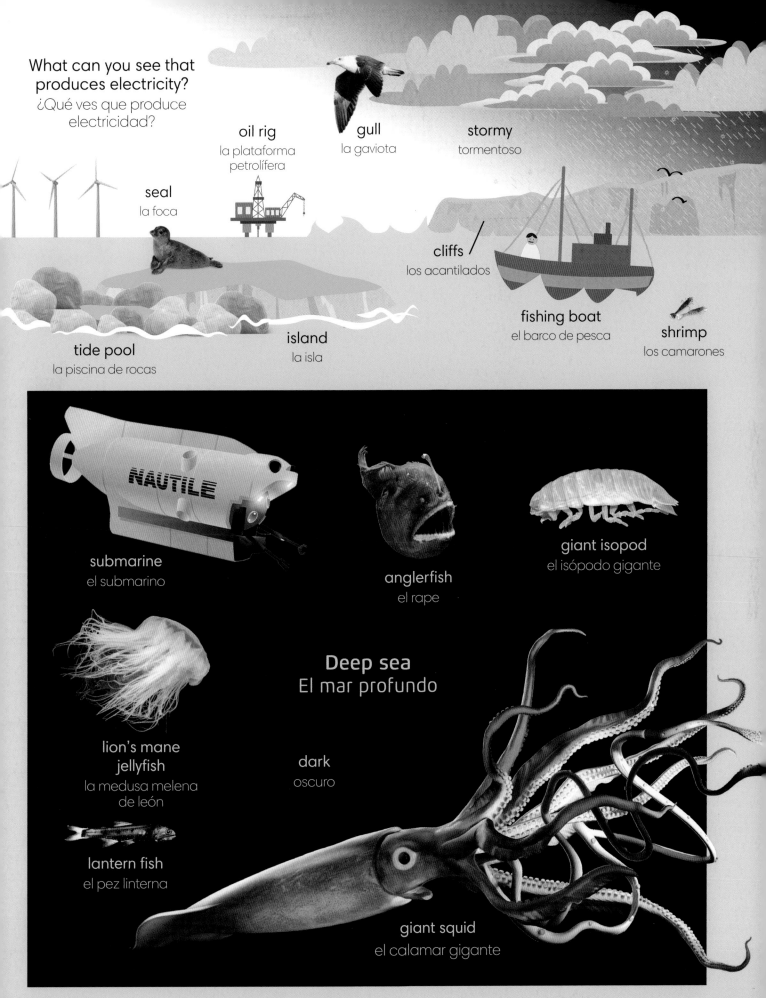

What can you see that produces electricity?
¿Qué ves que produce electricidad?

oil rig
la plataforma petrolífera

gull
la gaviota

stormy
tormentoso

seal
la foca

cliffs
los acantilados

fishing boat
el barco de pesca

shrimp
los camarones

tide pool
la piscina de rocas

island
la isla

submarine
el submarino

anglerfish
el rape

giant isopod
el isópodo gigante

lion's mane jellyfish
la medusa melena de león

Deep sea
El mar profundo

dark
oscuro

lantern fish
el pez linterna

giant squid
el calamar gigante

Rainforests
Las selvas tropicales

Many animal species live in rainforests, and there are lots of new species still to be discovered. Let's look at what lives in the Amazon rainforest of South America.

Muchas especies de animales viven en la selva tropical, y aún quedan muchas por descubrir. Vamos a ver quién vive en la selva amazónica de Sudamérica.

high
alto

sunny
soleado

capuchin monkey
el mono capuchino

kapok tree
la ceiba

climb
trepar

sloth
el perezoso

hang
colgarse

howler monkey
el mono aullador

vampire bat
el murciélago vampiro

Emergent layer
La capa emergente

harpy eagle
el águila harpía

glide
planear

blue morpho butterfly
la mariposa morfo azul

fly
volar

macaw
el guacamayo

tree boa
la boa arbórea

toucan
el tucán

green iguana
la iguana verde

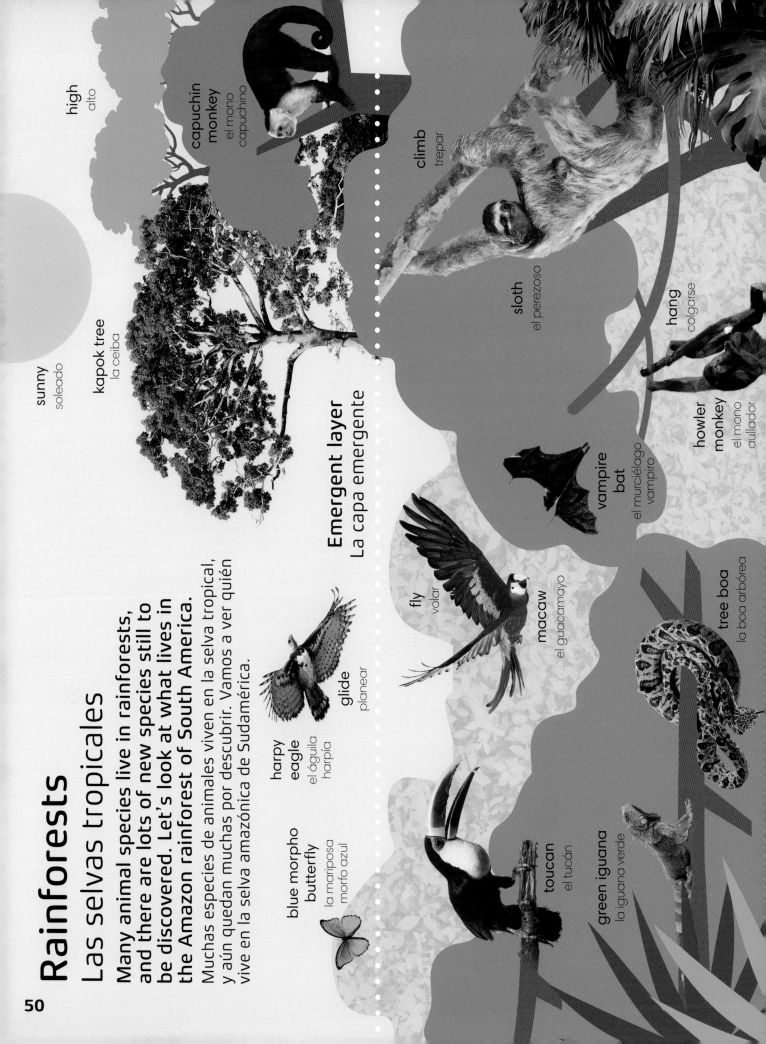

What sounds could you hear in a rainforest?
¿Qué sonidos escucharías en una selva tropical?

damp
húmedo

red-eyed
tree frog
la rana de ojos rojos

bananas
las bananas

nutrient
rich
rico en
nutrientes

fungi
los hongos

Canopy
El dosel

cocoa tree
el árbol del cacao

decay
la descomposición

buttress roots
las raíces de
soporte

jewel
beetle
el escarabajo
joya

orchid bee
la abeja de las orquídeas

cocoa pod
la vaina de cacao

jaguar
el jaguar

churo snail
el caracol churo

Understory
El sotobosque

Forest floor
El suelo del bosque

orchid
la orquídea

giant
centipede
el ciempiés
gigante

scorpion
el escorpión

leaf-cutter ant
la hormiga cortadora
de hojas

armadillo
el armadillo

harlequin
beetle
el aserrador
arlequín

giant
anteater
el oso hormiguero
gigante

Savannahs
Las sabanas

Savannahs are flat grasslands with few trees. There are often wildfires, but plants regrow. Some of the biggest savannahs are in Africa, South America, and Australia.

Las sabanas son praderas planas con pocos árboles. Es frecuente que haya incendios forestales, pero las plantas vuelven a crecer. Algunas de las mayores sabanas están en África, Sudamérica y Australia.

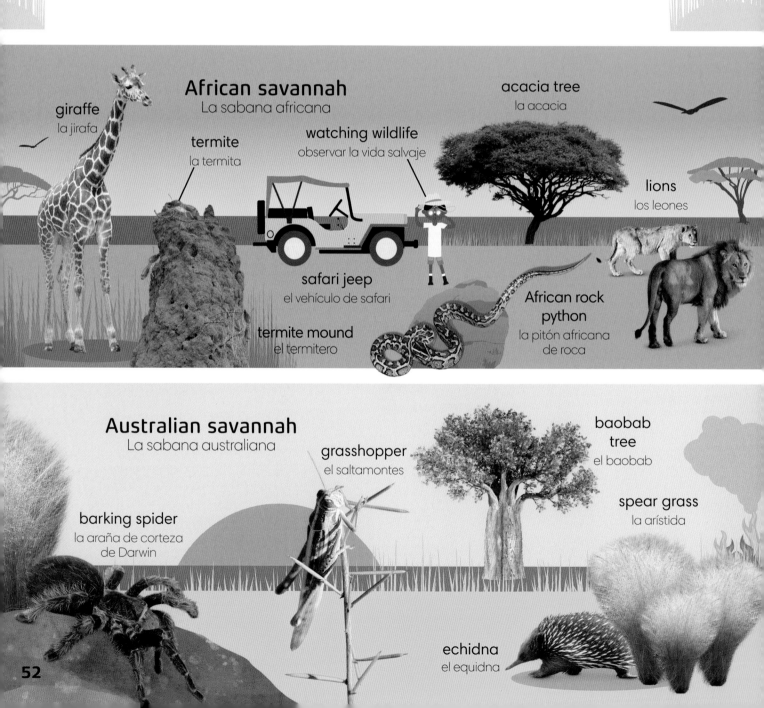

African savannah
La sabana africana

giraffe
la jirafa

termite
la termita

watching wildlife
observar la vida salvaje

acacia tree
la acacia

lions
los leones

safari jeep
el vehículo de safari

termite mound
el termitero

African rock python
la pitón africana de roca

Australian savannah
La sabana australiana

grasshopper
el saltamontes

baobab tree
el baobab

spear grass
la arístida

barking spider
la araña de corteza de Darwin

echidna
el equidna

South American savannah
La sabana sudamericana

pampas grass
la hierba de la pampa

rhea
el ñandú

pampas fox
el zorro pampeano

guinea pig
el conejillo de Indias

puma
el puma

footprints
las huellas

Which big mammal has a very long nose?
¿Qué gran mamífero tiene una nariz muy larga?

elephant dung
la caca de elefante

zebras
las cebras

impala
la impala

aardvark
el cerdo hormiguero

watering hole
la charca de agua

African elephant
el elefante africano

wildfire
el incendio forestal

screw pine
el pandano

eucalyptus
el eucalipto

dung beetle
el escarabajo pelotero

kangaroo
el canguro

frilled lizard
el dragón con volantes

possum
el pósum

bandicoot
el bandicut

Deserts
Los desiertos

Deserts can be hot or cold, but they all get very little rain. Let's look around the Chihuahuan Desert in Mexico.

Los desiertos pueden ser cálidos o fríos, pero en todos ellos llueve muy poco. Demos un vistazo al desierto de Chihuahua, en México.

red-tailed hawk
el gavilán colirrojo

hunt
cazar

Food chain
La cadena alimentaria

hiss
sisear

rattle
sonar

prickly pear cactus
el nopal

rattlesnake
la serpiente de cascabel

flow of nutrients
el flujo de los nutrientes

jackrabbit
la liebre

What eats what in the food chain?
¿Quién se come a quién en la cadena alimentaria?

tumbleweed
la planta rodadora

lizard
el lagarto

coyote
el coyote

desert kit fox
la zorrita del desierto

jaguar
el jaguar

dry
seco

barrel cactus
el cactus erizo

sand dune
la duna de arena

hot
cálido

Sun
el Sol

golden eagle
el águila real

arid
árido

grasshopper
el saltamontes

scorpion
el escorpión

dust storm
la tormenta
de polvo

bighorn sheep
el borrego cimarrón

sand
la arena

saguaro cactus
el saguaro

**Find three birds
and two reptiles.**
Encuentra tres aves
y dos reptiles.

roadrunner
el correcaminos

Joshua
tree
el árbol
de Josué

bobcat
el lince rojo

red-spotted toad
el sapo de puntos rojos

yucca
la yuca

aloe
la sábila

desert ants
las hormigas
del desierto

shade
la sombra

tarantula
la tarántula

55

Mountains
Las montañas

Mountains are towering lands of earth and stone. It gets colder as you go higher, so mountains are often snowy at the top.

Las montañas son moles imponentes de tierra y piedra. A medida que se sube, hace más frío, por lo que su cima suele estar nevada.

golden eagle
el águila real

snow
la nieve

cold
frío

sky
el cielo

pine
marten
la marta

mountain
goat
la cabra
blanca

hiking
senderismo

stone
la roca

hiking
boots
las botas de
montaña

foothill
la colina

lynx
el lince

wolf
el lobo

reindeer
el reno

red
squirrel
la ardilla
roja

cave
la cueva

bear cub
el osezno

Where could the mother
bear make her den?
¿Dónde podría la madre
oso hacer su guarida?

brown
bear
el oso pardo

cloud
la nube

summit
la cima

snowflakes
los copos
de nieve

peregrine falcon
el halcón peregrino

ski poles
los bastones
de esquí

ski
esquiar

frozen
helado

mountain
climber
el escalador

skier
el esquiador

rope
la cuerda

mountain
la montaña

tent
la tienda

cyclists
los ciclistas

camping
acampar

bicycle
la bicicleta

path
el camino

waterfall
la cascada

monarch
butterflies
las mariposas
monarca

fish
los peces

marmot
la marmota

plunge pool
la poza

rocks
las rocas

57

Arctic and Antarctic
El Ártico y la Antártida

Some amazing animals and plants have adapted to survive in the freezing polar habitats of the Arctic and the Antarctic.

Algunos animales y plantas se han adaptado para sobrevivir en los gélidos hábitats polares del Ártico y la Antártida.

The wildlife is different in each place. Do penguins live in the Arctic or the Antarctic?

La fauna es distinta en cada lugar. ¿Hay pingüinos tanto en el Ártico como en la Antártida?

Arctic
El Ártico

Arctic cotton grass
la hierba de algodón del Ártico

bog bilberry
el arándano ártico

grayleaf willow
el sauce ártico

reindeer lichen
el liquen de los renos

snowy owl
el búho nival

walrus
la morsa

Arctic tern
el charrán ártico

rocky coastline
la costa rocosa

Arctic fox
el zorro ártico

lemming
el lemming

reindeer
el reno

Arctic hare
la liebre ártica

beluga whale
la beluga

polar bear
el oso polar

harp seal
la foca pía

ice
el hielo

frozen
helado

narwhal
el narval

Antarctic
La Antártida

polar lights
la aurora polar

Antarctic
hair grass
la hierba pilosa
antártica

Antarctic
pearlwort
la perla antártica

peak
la cima

mountain
la montaña

wandering
albatross
el albatros
viajero

snow
la nieve

valley
el valle

snow petrel
el petrel níveo

iceberg
el iceberg

polar desert
el desierto polar

orca
la orca

adelie penguin
el pingüino de Adelia

krill
el kril

leopard seal
la foca leopardo

Weddell seal
la foca de Weddell

**Find three
Antarctic mammals.**
Encuentra tres mamíferos
antárticos.

emperor penguin
el pingüino emperador

starfish
la estrella de mar

gentoo penguin
el pingüino juanito

Protecting nature
Proteger la naturaleza

We should take care of our world. The choices we make can harm or protect nature.

Debemos cuidar nuestro mundo. Las decisiones que tomamos pueden dañar la naturaleza o protegerla.

Which of the things on these pages help protect nature?

¿Qué cosas de estas páginas ayudan a proteger la naturaleza?

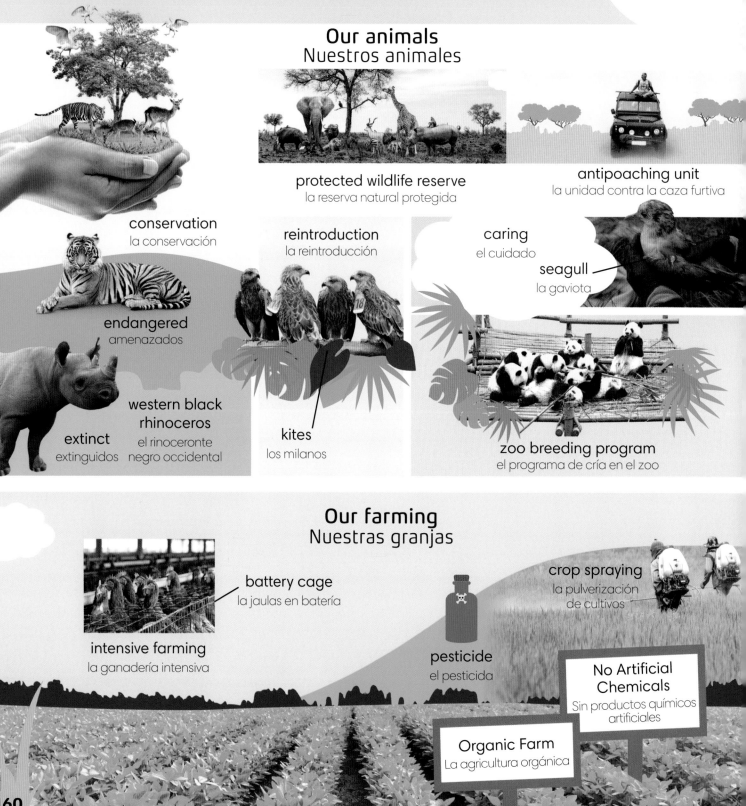

Our animals
Nuestros animales

protected wildlife reserve
la reserva natural protegida

antipoaching unit
la unidad contra la caza furtiva

conservation
la conservación

reintroduction
la reintroducción

caring
el cuidado

seagull
la gaviota

endangered
amenazados

western black rhinoceros
el rinoceronte negro occidental

extinct
extinguidos

kites
los milanos

zoo breeding program
el programa de cría en el zoo

Our farming
Nuestras granjas

battery cage
la jaulas en batería

crop spraying
la pulverización de cultivos

intensive farming
la ganadería intensiva

pesticide
el pesticida

No Artificial Chemicals
Sin productos químicos artificiales

Organic Farm
La agricultura orgánica

Our air
Nuestro aire

smog
la contaminación

air pollution
la contaminación
del aire

bicycling
ir en bicicleta

car sharing
compartir coche

electric bus
el autobús eléctrico

gas car
el coche de gasolina

electric car
el coche eléctrico

walking
caminar

Our trees
Nuestros árboles

deforestation
la deforestación

reforestation
la reforestación

Our climate
Nuestro clima

**global
warming**
el calentamiento
global

wildfires
los incendios forestales

floods
las inundaciones

**Reducing, reusing,
recycling**
Reducir, reutilizar,
reciclar

polar ice caps melting
el deshielo de los casquetes
polares

Can we do something
to help nature today?
¿Podemos hacer algo para
ayudar a la naturaleza?

Our oceans
Nuestros océanos

ocean litter
la basura en el mar

cleaning up
limpiar

Working with nature
Trabajar con la naturaleza

There are many ways to work with nature, including jobs in which you can help protect our planet and the species that live on it.

Hay muchas formas de trabajar con la naturaleza, incluidos los empleos en los que puedes ayudar a proteger nuestro planeta y las especies que viven en él.

air quality scientist: checks air pollution

la científica de calidad ambiental: comprueba la contaminación

farmer

la granjera

geologist: studies Earth's rocks

la geóloga: estudia las rocas de la Tierra

forester: takes care of forests

el guardabosques: se ocupa de los bosques

zoologist: studies animals

la zoóloga: estudia los animales

entomologist: studies insects

la entomóloga: estudia los insectos

environmental scientist: studies the environment

el científico medioambiental: estudia el medio ambiente

botanist: studies plants

el botánico: estudia las plantas

gardener

la jardinera

tree surgeon

el cirujano forestal

zookeeper

el cuidador del zoo

marine biologist: studies ocean life

el biólogo marino: estudia la vida del océano

vet
la veterinaria

environmental activist: supports protecting the environment
la activista medioambiental: apoya la protección del medio ambiente

natural history museum event manager
el responsable de eventos de un museo de historia natural

ecologist: studies living things and their environment
el ecólogo: estudia los seres vivos y su entorno

street cleaner
la limpiadora de calles

wildlife author
el autor de libros sobre la naturaleza

wildlife photographer
la fotógrafa de la naturaleza

aquarist: manages an aquarium
el acuarista: gestiona un acuario

park ranger: takes care of national parks
la guarda rural: cuida el campo

safari guide
el guía de safari

wildlife reporter
la presentadora de la vida salvaje

environmental engineer: designs things for the environment
la ingeniera ambiental: diseña cosas para el medio ambiente

animal-rescue worker
el trabajador de rescate de animales

seismologist: studies earthquakes
el sismólogo: estudia los terremotos

Which of these jobs would you like to do?
¿Cuál de estos trabajos te gustaría hacer?

63

Agradecimientos

DK quiere agradecer a: Victoria Palastanga y Eleanor Bates por su colaboración en el diseño; Jagtar Singh por su colaboración en las tareas de maquetación; Adhithi Priya, Sakshi Saluja, Rituraj Singh, Sumedha Chopra y Vagisha Pushp por su colaboración en los trabajos de documentación iconográfica, y Polly Goodman por la corrección.

Los editores agradecen a los siguientes su permiso para reproducir sus fotografías:

(Clave: a: arriba; b: bajo/debajo; c: centro; e: extremo; i: izquierda; d: derecha; s: superior)

1 123RF.com: Liubov Shirokova (cib); **Dreamstime.com:** Marc Bruxelle (cda); Isselee (sc); Vvoevale (si); Yinan Zhang (ci); Svetlana Larina / Blair_witch (ecib); Nejron (cb); Sabelskaya (bd). **2 Dorling Kindersley:** Tom Grey (cia); Natural History Museum, Londres (sd). **Getty Images / iStock:** photo5963 (cb). **3 123RF.com:** Isselee / Eric Isselee (bc); Prapan Ngawkeaw (cb/carretera); jackf / Iakov Filimonov (bi/lobo). **Dreamstime.com:** Iakov Filimonov (cib/cabra); Phartisan (roca x3); Jpsdk / Jens Stolt (mariposas x 3); Yotrak (cb/tienda); Jackf / Iakov Filimonov (bc/reno); Nelikz (bi/ardilla). **Shutterstock.com:** Aleksandr Pobedimskiy (cib/piedra arenisca). **6-7 Dreamstime.com:** Gritsalak Karalak (c). **6 Dreamstime.com:** Astrofireball (c). **7 Dorling Kindersley:** Dan Crisp (ca); Natural History Museum, Londres (si); James Kuether (cb); Jon Hughes (bc). **Dreamstime.com:** Nicolás Fernández (c); Markus Gann / Magann (cd). **8 123RF.com:** algre (cib). **Dreamstime.com:** Costasz (bc); Tomasz Śmigla (bc/tazas); Vchalup (bd); Rui Matos / Kolmat (cda); Rob Wilson / Robwilson39 (cd). **9 123RF.com:** julynx (ci); Martin Spurny (cia); Natthawut Panyosaeng / nopsan (ca). **Alamy Stock Photo:** Mouse in the House (bi). **Dreamstime.com:** Sergey Dzyuba (cd); Elena Kazanskaya (cia/cubo); Tele52 (cib); Radha Karuppannan / Radhuvenki (cib/x2); Stockphototrends (bd). **Getty Images / iStock:** DigitalVision Vectors / bubaone (c); photo5963 (ci); youngID (esi); pterwort (bd). **10 123RF.com:** Inna Astakhova (ci); tempusfugit (sc); nerthuz (bd). **Dorling Kindersley:** Tracy Morgan (cb/perro). **Dreamstime.com:** Melanie Hobson (ca/paisaje); Nexus7s (si); Isselee (ci); Theo Malings (cib); Eric Isselee (cd). **11 123RF.com:** Aaron Amat (cib/x3); Dmitry Rukhlenko / dimol (ecda). **Alamy Stock Photo:** Justin Kase z12z (ebi). **Dreamstime.com:** Billy Ber (sd); Narathip Ruksa / Narathip12 (esd); Cammeraydave (cb); Cynoclub (bc); Jeroen Van Den Broek / Vandenbroek29 (bc/perro guía); PhotoChur (bd); Zbynek Burival / Merial (ebd). **Fotolia:** Eric Isselee (bi); Norman Pogson (ca). **Getty Images / iStock:** Mac99 (ca); pifate (ci). **12 123RF.com:** fireflamenco (x3). **Dreamstime.com:** Catalin205 (cib, cdb); Vectorikart (bc); Stockoxinoxi (ca); Thomas Holt (ci); Macrovector (cib/red); Photka (bd). **13 Dreamstime.com:** Akinshin (sd); Vectorikart (ci); Andreanita (sd/oso); Miramisska (cda); Pavel Rodimov (c/observar las estrellas); Kotenko (c); Gerald Zaffuts (c/contar historias); Christinlola (cd); Sabelskaya (cib); Kellyrichardsonfl (bc); Pavel Naumov (cb/x4); Sergiy Bykhunenko (bd); Macrovector (ca). **14 Dreamstime.com:** Andreiuc88 (c); Antares614 (c); Nehru (bd). **15 123RF.com:** Rune Kristoffersen (ca). **Dreamstime.com:** Mihai Andritoiu (cd); Mishoo (si); Artisticco Llc (cd). **16 123RF.com:** justoomm (bc); Kitsadakron Pongha (cda); nasaimages (c/ciclón). **Alamy Stock Photo:** Mike Hill (c). **Dreamstime.com:** Arevhamb (bi); Andrey Armyagov (cia); Hulv850627 (ci); Justin Hobson (cd); Trekandshoot (cib); Thescv (cib); Elantsev (ci); Ruthchoi (bd). **17 123RF.com:** alicenerr (c). **Alamy Stock Photo:** SPUTNIK (ci). **Dreamstime.com:** Giuseppe Di Paolo (ca); Siempreverde22 (cia); Dmitry Pichugin / Dmitryp (ca/Everest); Valore (ci); Unissunil (c/Mawsynram); Jon Chica Parada (cd). **Getty Images:** Daniel Osterkamp (c). **Getty Images / iStock:** Jorge Villalba (ci). **18 123RF.com:** Ruth Jenkinson / stevanzz (bi); Andrzej Tokarski / ajt (sc); Przemyslaw Koch (ecib). **Dorling Kindersley:** Liberty's Owl, Raptor and Reptile Centre, Hampshire, UK (cib); Thomas Palmer (cb). **Dreamstime.com:** Digitalimagined (cib/hepática); Anna Sedneva / Sedneva (cib/hierba); Vital (c); Sarah2 (cdb/garrapata); Ildar Galeev (bc). **Fotolia:** Karl Bolf (ecdb). **Getty Images / iStock:** Antagain (cib). **19 123RF.com:** smileus (sc); Pavlo Vakhrushev / vapi (cia); Ten Theeralerttham / rawangtak (ci); Thawat Tanhai (bi). **Dreamstime.com:** Conchasdiver (cib); Igor Dolgov / Id1974 (sc); Ronniechua (c); Kotomiti_okuma (cib); Kazoka (cd). **20 Dreamstime.com:** Cherdchai Chaivimol (cb/brote); Vaclav Volrab (ca); Kaiwut Niponkaew (ca); Tomboy2290 (cda/albahaca); Natali572 (ca); Ppy2010ha (cib); Dewins (bc); Lepas (bi); Oleg Dudko (bi); Bogdan Lazar (cb); Songyuth Unkong (sb); Mikhail Dudarev (bd). **21 123RF.com:** Anna Liebiedieva / utima (ci); olegdudko (c/Kiwi). **Dorling Kindersley:** Neil Fletcher (cb). **Dreamstime.com:** Anton Ignatenco (c); Zerbor (cia); David Ridley (esi); Paul Rookes (ci); Zerbor (ecia); Natika (cib); Elena Schweitzer / Egal (cib); Roman Ivaschenko (bi); Roman Ivaschenko (bi/algas); Vetre Antanaviciute-meskauskiene (c). **Getty Images / iStock:** DNY59 (ecda). **Shutterstock.com:** Daydreamr Digital Studio (sd). **22 Dorling Kindersley:** Centre for Wildlife Gardening / London Wildlife Trust (ca). **Dreamstime.com:** Marc Bruxelle (ci); Vvoevale (cia); Pipa100 (cib); Dreamstock (bi); Filmfoto (bi); Anatoliy Mandrichenko (bc). **22-23 Dreamstime.com:** Andreykuzmin (bi); Zerbor (c). **23 Dreamstime.com:** Denira777 (cda); Anton Ignatenco (sd); Ievgenii Tryfonov (bc); Setory (bd); Majormetts (cib); Zorica Vitanovic (ca). **24 Dreamstime.com:** Domnitsky (ca); Md. Rakibul Hassan (ciclo de vida del girasol); Ilonai (sd). **25 Dreamstime.com:** Elena Elisseeva (cd); Nadiia Havryliuk Kharzhevska (bi/ciclo de las setas); Luayana (si/ciclo del manzano); Angelo Gilardelli (sd); Lenazajchikova (cib); Pavel Rodimov (bd); Wirestock (cib); Thawats (cia). **26 123RF.com:** Aleksandr Ermolaev (cd). **Dreamstime.com:** Anankkml (bc); Photodeti (ca); Wirestock (bd). **Fotolia:** Mark Higgins (ebd). **Getty Images / iStock:** LUNAMARINA (bi). **27 Alamy Stock Photo:** Islandstock (bc). **Dreamstime.com:** Jason W. Baker (si); Isselee (cada); Svetlana Larina / Blair_witch (sd); Pimmimemom (ci); Stevenrussellsmithphotos (ca, ecia); Vasiliy Vishnevskiy (cib); Cinnamongirl (cib). **Science Photo Library:** Claude Nuridsany & Marie Perennou (ci). **Shutterstock.com:** Lamnoi Manas (cib). **28 123RF.com:** Anna Utekhina (bc). **Dreamstime.com:** Accept001 (si); Isselee (bc/dálmata); Judith Dzierzawa (bd); Alexander Potapov (cib/oveja); Alexander Potapov (cada); Isselee (cib/vaca); Tristana / Kseniya Abramova (ca); Isselee (bia). **Fotolia:** Anatolii (ci); Olena Pantiukh (cib). **Getty Images:** mikroman6 (ci). **29 123RF.com:** Cathy Keifer (sc); smileus (sd). **Alamy Stock Photo:** Lee Dalton (ci). **Dorling Kindersley:** British Wildlife Centre, Surrey, UK (cia). **Dreamstime.com:** Linda Caldwell (ci); Toby Gibson (bc); Dizzizzmee (ca); Paul Farnfield (ecia); Steve Oehlenschlager (si); Brett Hondow (sc/tarántula). **Fotolia:** Eric Isselee (c). **Getty Images:** Photodisc / Don Farrall (esi). **30 123RF.com:** Visarute Angkatavanich (bd). **Dreamstime.com:** Adogslifephoto (cia); Sutisa Kangvansap (bc); Prin Pattawaro (bi); Graeme Snow (cib); Billybruce2000 (cib); Marcin Wojciechowski (cd); Joanna Zopoth Lipiejko (c); Sonsedskaya (ci); Isselee (cda); Gianluca Piccin (ca). **Getty Images:** RAUSINPHOTO (cib). **31 Dreamstime.com:** Mira Agron (eci); Sebastian Kaulitzki (bd); Pavel Trankov (bc); Steve Allen (bi); Isselee (cda); Isselee (cib); Isselee (cib); Gualberto Becerra (cd); Marco Tomasini (ci); Duncan Noakes (ecda); Wrangel (cda); Melinda Fawver (ca); Svetlana Foote (cia); Dirk Ercken (ecia); Jacoba Susanna Maria Swanepoel (ci); Wildlife World (si); Jagodka (sc); Alexandercreator (si); Reimarg (esi). **32 123RF.com:** ksena32 / Oksana Tkachuk (cda/camomila). **Alamy Stock Photo:** Jason Bazzano (bi); mauritius images GmbH / Kurt Madersbacher (ci). **Dreamstime.com:** Andreanita (ca); José Manuel Gelpi Díaz (cda/buitre); Valentyna Chukhlyebova (ca, ci); Hwongcc (cia, c); Golfxx (ci); Marazem (bc); Dmitry Potashkin (bi); Pop Nukoonrat (cielo). **33 Dreamstime.com:** Kharis Agustiar (cd); Jocrebbin (bc); Zedcreations / SACHITH (redes x2); Geerati (ca); Duncan Noakes (cia). **Getty Images:** The Image Bank / Joe McDonald (bi). **Getty Images / iStock:** Parrotstarr (cib); superjoseph (ca); pixhook (ca/bambú). **34 123RF.com:** Isselee Eric Philippe (c). **Alamy Stock Photo:** Arterra Picture Library / Clement Philippe (bc). **Dreamstime.com:** Callipso88 (cd); Vasyl Helevachuk (bi); Dizm (cb); Isselee (cib); Wildlife World (ca); Corey A Ford (cia). **Getty Images:** Photodisc / Don Farrall (ca). **Shutterstock.com:** A.Mac.Photo (ci). **35 123RF.com:** John McAllister (ci); utima (ca). **Alamy Stock Photo:** Bill Coster (c); Pally (bd); Les Gibbon (bi). **Dreamstime.com:** Ángel Luis Simón Martín (cib); Sergeyoch (cib). **Getty Images:** Hearst Newspapers / San Francisco Chronicle (cda). **Getty Images / iStock:** LuckyTD (ci). **36 123RF.com:** swavo (bd); Andrzej Tokarski / ajt (ci). **Dorling Kindersley:** Natural History Museum, Londres (ci). **Dreamstime.com:** Isselee (cdb); Alexander Konoplyov (bd/bacterias); Stu Porter (ca); Mrrphotography (si). **Getty Images / iStock:** bbevren (b). **37 123RF.com:** Eric Isselee (bc). **Ardea:** ar / Science Source / Tom McHugh (ci). **Dorling Kindersley:** Natural History Museum, Londres (ci); Jerry Young (bi); Wildlife Heritage Foundation, Kent, UK (si). **Dreamstime.com:** Isselee (cib); Jblackstock / Justin Black (cib); Yves Sautter (c/pulpo). **38 123RF.com:** Nchuprin / Andrey Sukhachev (cdb/bacteria); Angelique Nijssen (bi); Thatsaphon Saengnarongrat (sd). **38-39 Dreamstime.com:** Andreykuzmin (soil); Smishko (textura de arena). **39 123RF.com:** Sayompu Chamnankit (bc/huellas). **Alamy Stock Photo:** Rosanne Tackaberry (bc). **Dorling Kindersley:** Dreamstime.com: Andreykuzmin (b); Dijarm (bd/gráfico); Kosmos111 (cib); Сергей Кучугурный (bi); Tamara Kulikova (ci); Hommalai (sc); Dave Nelson (ca); Thanthip Homsansri (cia); Lcrms7 (ci); Sripfoto (ci); Typsiaod (cib). **Shutterstock.com:** Mikkola (cd). **40 123RF.com:** alekss / Alexandr Pakhnyushchyy (bi); Anatolii Tsekhmister (cia). **Alamy Stock Photo:** Don Despain (ci). **Dorling Kindersley:** Dreamstime.com: Chernetskaya (ecdb); Uros Petrovic (bd); Pzaxe (bc); Loren File (cib); Ivonne Wierink (ecdb/macetas); Jagade (cia). **Shutterstock.com:** Artiste2d3d (ecda). **41 Dreamstime.com:** Nikolay Antonov (cib/lombriz); Kristof Lauwers (bd); Pimmimemom (ci); Aleksandr Volkov (cib); Fibobjects (cib); Luceluceluce (cib/tierra); Atlasfotoreception (cdb/guantes); Boulanger Sandrine (cd); Bundit Minramun (cia); Sergiy1975 (ci/cortacésped). **42-43 Dreamstime.com:** Miriam Doerr (flor x3); Eugenesergeev (hierba); Miriam Doerr (flores silvestres x3); Supertrooper (c). **42 123RF.com:** peterwaters (cdb/abeja). **Alamy Stock Photo:** Isselee on white (cia/caballo). **Dorling Kindersley:** Mark Hamblin (c). **Dreamstime.com:** Animaflora (cib); Tazzymoto (ca); Brett Critchley (ca); Isselee (c); Dzmitry Shpak (ecdb); Inna Kyselova (cib); Nipaporn Panyacharoen (cb/cebada); Thawats (bc). **Shutterstock.com:** Volosina (cib). **43 Alamy Stock Photo:** Islandstock (ca). **Dorling Kindersley:** Twan Leenders (cb/serpiente). **Dreamstime.com:** Tony Bosse (si); Mickem (bc); Tchara (cb); Chuyu (cib); Sandra Standbridge (cib); Isselee (c); Romica (cda); Palians (cda/cosechadora); Mariya Kondratyeva (cda/tierra). **44 123RF.com:** Eric Isselee (c). **Alamy Stock Photo:** Imagebroker / Arco / J. Fieber (bi). **Dorling Kindersley:** Roger Tidman (c). **Dreamstime.com:** ActiveLines; Macrovector (ci); Isselee (cdb); Stephanie Frey (ci); Zerbor (c); Atman (sc); Mille19 (cib/búho). **Getty Images / iStock:** MarkMirror (c). **45 123RF.com:** Eric Isselee (cda/koala). **Dreamstime.com:** Karen Black (cda); Alexander Potapov (bc); Susan Sheldon (bi); Geoffrey Kuchera (bi/oso); Donyanedomam (cib); Lunamarina (cia); David Steele (ca). **Getty Images / iStock:** GlobalP (cib). **Shutterstock.com:** aphotostory (cib). **46-47 Dreamstime.com:** David Watson (bc). **Shutterstock.com:** xpixel (caño x5). **46 123RF.com:** Stanko Mravljak (cdb/efímera). **Dreamstime.com:** G3miller / Gordon Miller (c); Zerbor (sd); Eduard Kyslynskyy (ca); Dennis Jacobsen (c); Kevin Wells (cb); Photophreak (cib); Roman Ivaschenko (bc). **Shutterstock.com:** Igor Podgorny (ca). **47 123RF.com:** Stefan Holm (cib/libélula); NewAge (ci). **Dorling Kindersley:** Roger Tidman (c). **Dreamstime.com:** Natalya Aksenova (ci); Sova004 (bd); Ilyas Kalimullin (cib); Kobchaima (cda); Wirestock (sd); Jnjhuz (cib); Zeytun Images (ci). **44 123RF.com:** Isselee (cib). **48-49 Getty Images / iStock:** photo5963 (ca). **48 Alamy Stock Photo:** Doug Perrine (cd); SBS Eclectic Images (cb); Carsten Reisinger (cd); WaterFrame_dpr (cib). **Dorling Kindersley:** Natural History Museum, Londres (bi); Linda Pitkin (ci). **Dreamstime.com:** Kevin Panizza (ecib); Pipa100 (cb/lechuga); Harvey Stowe (cda). **Fotolia:** uwimages (cdb/anémona de mar). **49 123RF.com:** feathercollector (cd). **Alamy Stock Photo:** Minden Pictures / Norbert Wu (c). **Dorling Kindersley:** Tom Grey (sc). **Dreamstime.com:** Robertlasalle (ci). **naturepl.com:** Solvin Zankl (cib/rape). **50-51 Dreamstime.com:** Surachet Khamsuk. **50 123RF.com:** Hal Brindley (sc); Hal Brindley (ecda). **Alamy Stock Photo:** Ivan Kuzmin (si); Nature Picture Library / MYN / Andrew Snyder (cib); Nature Picture Library / Nick Garbutt (cb/águila). **Dreamstime.com:** Carlosphotos (sc); Nejron (cdb); Chansom Pantip (esd); Arindam Ghosh (ca). **naturepl.com:** Luiz Claudio Marigo (ca). **51 123RF.com:** anankkml / Anan Kaewkhammul (cb/jaguar); Ajay Bhaskar (d). **Alamy Stock Photo:** Zizza Gordon Insect collection (bi). **Dreamstime.com:** Beautifulblossom (sd); Ryszard Laskowski (bc); Gan Chaonan (bd); Whiskybottle (bc/orquídea); Isselee (cib); Olga Soe (flores rojas x3); Thenatureguy1 (cib); Morley Read (cdb/escorpión); Vlad Ivantcov (c); Superoke (cib); Douglas Delgado (cdb); Ekays (si); Waraphot Wapakphet (si/hojas). **naturepl.com:** Gabriel Rojo (cib). **52 123RF.com:** waldemarus (bc/baobab). **Dreamstime.com:** Bennymarty (cb); Yinan Zhang (sc); Snehitdesign (c); Alexander Shalamov (cd); Kewuwu (c/árbol); Fritz Hiersche (bc); Svetlana485 (bd); Alexandr Yurtchenko (ci). **naturepl.com:** Piotr Naskrecki (cib/hormiga 1, cib/hormiga 2, cib/hormiga 3). **53 Alamy Stock Photo:** Ken Griffiths (bd). **Dorling Kindersley:** Blackpool Zoo (cib); Wildlife Heritage Foundation, Kent, UK (cd). **Dreamstime.com:** Anekoho (cd); Lev Kropotov (cib); Pokec / Jan Pokornik (cib); Birdiegal717 (bc); Izanbar (bc/possum); Godruma (bi); Johan63 / Johannes Gerhardus Swanepoel (cd); Luca Santilli (ci); Vicspacewalker (cib); Luciano Queiroz (ci); Rafael Cerqueira (cia/conejillo de Indias). **54 123RF.com:** cookelma (ci); Andrey Armyagov (b); Anan Kaewkhammul / anankkml (bd). **Alamy Stock Photo:** George Brice (bi); Robert Shantz (cd); Mike Lane (cda). **Dorling Kindersley:** Andy and Gill Swash (cd). **Dreamstime.com:** Steve Byland (si); Derrick Neill (cib); Eutoch (ecd); Eutoch (ecib); Natalie Ruffing (cd); sladerer / Scott Laderer (ca); Ufuk Zivana (ca/cactus). **Alamy Stock Photo:** Arterra Picture Library / Clement Philippe (bc); Stu Porter (cdb); John Abbott (b); Rick & Nora Bowers (cib). **55 123RF.com:** alhovik (ecda); Natalie Ruffing (cd). **Dreamstime.com:** Dfikar (cib); Frank Fichtmueller (ecdb); Skynetphoto (cib); Domnitsky (c); Withgod / Alexander Podshivalov (si); Vally (cia). **56-57 Dreamstime.com:** Phartisan (roca x4). **56-57 Shutterstock.com:** Aleksandr Pobedimskiy (bd/caliza x2). **56 123RF.com:** jackf / Iakov Filimonov (bc). **Alamy Stock Photo:** Niebrugge Images (bd); Paulette Sinclair (cib/oso); Ronald S Phillips (bc). **Dreamstime.com:** Jim Cumming (cda); Jackf / Iakov Filimonov (si); Iakov Filimonov (bc). **57 123RF.com:** Isselee / Eric Isselee (cib); Prapan Ngawkeaw (c). **Dreamstime.com:** Jpsdk / Jens Stolt (mariposas x3); Yotrak (cib). **Shutterstock.com:** Yes058 Montree Nanta (bd/granito). **58 Alamy Stock Photo:** All Canada Photos / Wayne Lynch (ecib); Dembinsky Photo Associates / Alamy / Dominique Braud (si); Bob Gibbons (ca); Realimage (cia). **Dorling Kindersley:** Jerry Young (ci). **Dreamstime.com:** Devon Crosby (bi); Planetfelicity (bd); Luna Vandoorne Vallejo (c); Grafner (b); Outdoorsman (ecdb); Uhg1234 (cib/reno); Zanskar / Vladimir Melnik (ci). **Getty Images / iStock:** Luis Leamus (cd); Il'mar Idiyatullin (ecda); Troyka (ca). **Getty Images / iStock:** Karyn Schiller (c). **59 Alamy Stock Photo:** ere-images / Colin Harris (c); Minden Pictures / Norbert Wu (c). **Dreamstime.com:** Agami Photo Agency (cia); Photographerlondon (bd); Sharon Jones (cib); Vika Ivanets (cb); Freezingpictures / Jan Martin Will (cd); Slowmotiongli (c); Staphy (ca); Biletskiy (s); Viktoria Ivanets (sc). **Getty Images:** Digital Vision / David Tipling (bi). **60 Alamy Stock Photo:** Roger Hutchings (ca); WhiskeyWolf (ci); Ann and Steve Toon (c). **Dreamstime.com:** Adogslifephoto (ci); Chuchart Duangdaw (cib); Comzeal (cib); Hel080808 (cd); Nilangan Bhattacharya (cia/tigre); Maxirf (cda/unidad contra la caza furtiva); Sarayut Thaneerat (cib). **61 Dreamstime.com:** Steve Allen (bc); Skylightpictures (cd); Andrey Koturanov (cib/inundación); David Pereiras Villagra (bd); Romolo Tavani (cib); Win Nondakowit (b); Gpgroup (cib); Sjors737 (cda); Piotr Wawrzyniuk (cia); Noamfein (ci). **64 Dreamstime.com:** Marc Bruxelle (sd/arce); Vvoevale (sd); Nadiia Havryliuk Kharzhevska (cib); Zerbor (sd/arce)

Imágenes de la cubierta: *Frontal y contracubierta:* **Dreamstime.com:** Irinav; *Frontal:* **123RF.com:** Aaron Amat bc/ (avestruz); jackf / Iakov Filimonov ci; madllen (brote), Liubov Shirokova (flor), Andrzej Tokarski / ajt ebd, Anatolii Tsekhmister (ardilla); **Dorling Kindersley:** Blackpool Zoo cia, Centre for Wildlife Gardening / London Wildlife Trust (hoja de acebo), Mark Hamblin tc, Liberty's Owl, Raptor and Reptile Centre, Hampshire, UK (tarántula), Natural History Museum, Londres (mariposa), Jerry Young (abejorro); **Dreamstime.com:** Atman (hoja), Marc Bruxelle (hoja de arce), Carlosphotos (mariposa x 2), Denira777 cd, Igor Dolgov / Id1974 cda, Dreamstock (abeto), Dvrcan cda/ (gorgojo), Iakov Filimonov cia/ (cabra), Angelo Gilardelli (bd), Godruma ca/ (escarabajo), Vasyl Helevachuk (petirrojo), Eric Isselee (gusano de seda), Isselee (ciervo), Jblackstock / Justin Black sd, Jgade (rana), Johan63 / Johannes Gerhardus Swanepoel (impala), Svetlana Larina / Blair_witch cib, Nejron (loro), Matee Nuserm ecdb, Pokec / Jan Pokornik (cib/ (canguro), Stu Porter (guepardo), Ievgenii Tryfonov ci/ (tronco), Vasiliy Vishnevskiy cb/ (grajo), Vvoevale (hoja seca); **Getty Images:** Fuse cb/ (jaguar); **Getty Images / iStock:** GlobalP si, igorkv (águila); *Back:* **123RF.com:** madllen (brote), Liubov Shirokova (flor), Anatolii Tsekhmister (ardilla); **Dorling Kindersley:** Jerry Young (pez espinoso), Centre for Wildlife Gardening / London Wildlife Trust (hoja de acebo), Twan Leenders si, Liberty's Owl, Raptor and Reptile Centre, Hampshire, UK (tarántula), Natural History Museum, Londres (mariposa), Jerry Young (abejorro); **Dreamstime.com:** Atman (hoja), Marc Bruxelle (hoja de arce), Dreamstock (abeto), Dvrcan (gorgojo), Freezingpictures / Jan Martin Will (pingüino), Vasyl Helevachuk (petirrojo), Eric Isselee (gusano de seda), Isselee (reno), Jgade (rana), Johan63 / Johannes Gerhardus Swanepoel (impala), Svetlana Larina / Blair_witch ca, Luis Leamus cd, Nejron (loro), Uros Petrovic cdb, Stu Porter (guepardo), Ievgenii Tryfonov (tronco), Vasiliy Vishnevskiy (roca), Vvoevale (hoja seca), Zerbor bc; **Getty Images / iStock:** GlobalP (panda), igorkv (águila); *Lomo:* **Dreamstime.com:** Macrovector (caracol), Alexander Potapov (agárico)

Resto de las imágenes: © Dorling Kindersley
Para más información ver: www.dkimages.com